Division of Research
Work Projects Administration

Research Monographs

A Da Capo Press Reprint Series

**FRANKLIN D. ROOSEVELT
AND THE ERA OF THE NEW DEAL**
GENERAL EDITOR: FRANK FREIDEL
Harvard University

VOCATIONAL TRAINING
AND EMPLOYMENT
OF YOUTH

Works Progress Administration
Division of Social Research
Research Monograph XXV

VOCATIONAL TRAINING AND EMPLOYMENT OF YOUTH

By Selden C. Menefee

DA CAPO PRESS • NEW YORK • 1971

A Da Capo Press Reprint Edition

This Da Capo Press edition of *Vocational Training and Employment of Youth* is an unabridged republication of the first edition published in Washington, D.C., in 1942. It is reprinted by permission from a copy of the original edition owned by the Harvard College Library.

Library of Congress Catalog Card Number 70-166953
ISBN 0-306-70357-2

Published by Da Capo Press, Inc.
A Subsidiary of Plenum Publishing Corporation
227 West 17th Street, New York, N.Y. 10011
All Rights Reserved

Manufactured in the United States of America

VOCATIONAL TRAINING
AND EMPLOYMENT
OF YOUTH

FEDERAL WORKS AGENCY

Major General Philip B. Fleming, *Administrator*

WORK PROJECTS ADMINISTRATION

George H. Field, *Deputy Commissioner*

DIVISION OF RESEARCH

Howard B. Myers, *Director*

VOCATIONAL TRAINING AND EMPLOYMENT OF YOUTH

By

Selden C. Menefee

Under the Supervision of

John N. Webb

Chief, Labor Market Research Section
Division of Research

•

RESEARCH MONOGRAPH XXV

1942

UNITED STATES GOVERNMENT PRINTING OFFICE WASHINGTON

Letter of Transmittal

WORK PROJECTS ADMINISTRATION,
Washington, D. C., December 1, 1941.

SIR: I transmit herewith an analysis of public school vocational training in relation to the employment of youth. The report is based upon interviews with more than 3,000 youth who had received some full-time training under the provisions of the Smith-Hughes Act, the basic law providing for Federal assistance to vocational schools.

Vocational training has an essential function to perform in modern society: the providing of trained workers for jobs in factories, shops, and offices. The public school system is not the only agency charged with the responsibility of replenishing the Nation's supply of skilled workers. Private schools, apprenticeship plans sponsored by unions and employers, WPA defense training projects, and industrial training plans of various sorts also make their contributions to the skilled labor supply. But as the apprenticeship system has declined in recent years, and as new types of jobs have been created by modern technology, the public vocational schools have played an increasingly important part in supplying the need for trained workers.

The unprecedented demand for trained workers created by the defense program has already resulted in the enrollment of several millions of persons in vocational training classes. The rapid expansion of defense training programs has been seriously handicapped, however, by the lack of adequate research aimed at evaluating the effectiveness of vocational training. In presenting such an evaluation the present report makes an important contribution to the defense effort.

This study, which was an offshoot of a more comprehensive survey of youth in the labor market, was originally undertaken because of the marked interest shown by educators, employers, and youth themselves in vocational education and its results. An even greater interest in vocational training has been manifested since the defense program has created a demand for certain types of skilled labor. The WPA has recently established a Division of Training and Reemployment in order to train its workers for, and place them in, defense industries. The present report is designed to meet the need for additional information through an appraisal of the results of federally aided vocational training as it has operated in the past.

The data presented in the report indicate that vocational training under the standards set up by the Smith-Hughes Act has had considerable effectiveness in channeling the economic activities of youth in the intended directions, but that it leaves much to be desired. Its shortcomings are suggested by the facts that a large number of trained youth had never obtained jobs in their fields of training; that there was great variation among programs (courses of study) in terms of the proportions of youth getting jobs related to the fields in which they had been trained; and that trained youth were at about the same level as youth with no Smith-Hughes training as far as total employment and earnings were concerned. The report not only analyzes the accomplishments of full-time Smith-Hughes vocational training, but also attempts to evaluate some of the factors underlying the success or failure of trained youth in finding employment in their fields of training.

The study is based on the status of trained youth on July 1, 1938, and their experiences during the depression years prior to that date. While a survey of the same youth made today might show somewhat different results, it is felt that the general picture of the effects of vocational training as presented in the report remains valid.

The report should be of value to all those who are interested in vocational training in relation to youth, the public schools, and the defense program. The Work Projects Administration is concerned with this question not only because approximately one-tenth of all project workers are youth under 25 years of age, and because of the necessity for training or retraining persons of all ages who are still dependent on work relief, but also because defense training projects in which many WPA workers have been and are being trained use public school facilities which were installed and used for Smith-Hughes vocational courses of the sort under discussion.

The report should be of considerable interest to teachers in secondary institutions where vocational training of the Smith-Hughes type is offered. Vocational guidance counselors should also find the study to be of value in their work, since it may help them to reduce the length of the "floundering period" through which urban youth often pass before making satisfactory occupational adjustments.

The study was made by the Division of Research under the direction of Howard B. Myers, Director of the Division. The data were analyzed and the report was prepared by Selden C. Menefee, under the supervision of John N. Webb, Chief of the Labor Market Research Section. Special acknowledgment is made to Wayne F. Daugherty, who assisted in planning the tabulation of the data, to Beatrice Mathieson and Lucille Maupin, who assisted in preparing the data for analysis, and to Stanley L. Payne and Albert Westefeld, who read and criticized the manuscript.

Respectfully submitted.

HOWARD B. MYERS,
Director of Research.

Contents

V.

ILLUSTRATIONS
Figure   **Figures**

Vocational Training and Employment of Youth

INTRODUCTION

THE NATIONAL defense program, with its far-reaching plans for the training of skilled workers, has focused much attention upon our public school system of vocational education. With shortages of certain types of skilled craftsmen reported in many localities, there is an increasing demand for a large-scale training program for youth. The form which such a program may take is of direct concern to WPA, since its project workers comprise the largest single reserve supply of employable labor, and since these workers must be prepared to fill the needs of private industry for trained labor as rapidly as possible during the defense period.

Yet comparatively little is known about the actual results of vocational training in terms of its past effectiveness in fitting youth for jobs. Are our present training facilities adequate for turning out the skilled workers who may be needed in industry? And does vocational training help youth to become adjusted in an overcrowded labor market? The best way of answering these questions is to examine the work histories of youth who have had full-time training under the federally sponsored program in the past few years, to determine how many have actually used that training. The results of such an examination have an important bearing on the whole problem of unemployment among youth.

THE GENERAL PROBLEM

America's unemployed may, for purposes of analysis, be conveniently divided into three groups: youth under 25, who comprised 36 percent of all unemployed persons in 1937; workers supposedly at their peak of efficiency, from 25 through 44, who made up 37 percent of the unemployed group; and older workers, 45 years of age or over, who constituted 27 percent of the total number of persons unemployed.[1] Of these three groups youth and older workers face the

---

[1] Dedrick, Calvert L. and Hansen, Morris H., *Final Report on Total and Partial Unemployment, 1937: The Enumerative Check Census*, Vol. IV, Census of Partial Employment, Unemployment, and Occupations, Washington, D. C., 1938, table 4, p. 12.

most serious problems: youth because they lack maturity, experience, and training, and older workers because their skills are outmoded or because of the reluctance of industry to hire persons who may soon reach the age of physical disability or retirement.

The question of jobs for unemployed youth is in some respects the most pressing aspect of our unemployment problem. When almost a third of all youth in the labor market are unemployed, as was the case as recently as March 1940,[2] there is a danger not only that the strength and energies of these youth may be wasted, but also that their morale will suffer. Since productive man power is one of our greatest and most essential national resources, and since young men and women are the source of the Nation's labor supply, it is essential that unemployment among youth be reduced to a minimum.

Prior to the depression the transition from school to employment was often hampered by rapid technological developments in certain industries, minor cycles of business activity, or seasonal variations in employment. But in an expanding economy the great majority of youth were able somehow to get a start in business or industry. For the past decade, however, youth have had great difficulty in bridging the gap between school and jobs. Contracting business activity has resulted in the dismissal of many experienced workers, and young people who have just left school have found it difficult to compete with them for jobs. To make matters worse, the largest crop of youth America has yet produced came of working age during the depression, with the result that the labor force increased by a net total of about 6 million persons from 1929 to 1939.

Some youth stayed in school to postpone the discouraging task of hunting employment under depression conditions. Those who found a place in the economic structure were confronted by low wage scales and limited opportunities for advancement. Enforced idleness and dead-end jobs took their toll of youthful enthusiasm; marriage and normal family life were postponed; and America began to hear from all sides that it had a "youth problem" on its hands.

---

[2] "The burden of unemployment in March 1940 was especially heavy on youth just out of school. Less than 70 percent of the boys and girls 14 to 19 years old who had joined the labor force were employed at nonrelief jobs, while 23 percent of the boys and 26 percent of the girls were entirely without work and looking for a job. The older youth, in the age class 20 to 24 years, fared better, no doubt because they had more work experience and better training, but even at this age 20 percent of the male and 15 percent of the female workers were either out of a job and looking for work or reported that they were on emergency work projects. Unemployment rates for adult workers over 25 years old were only about half as great." Bureau of the Census, *The Facts About Youth* as *Portrayed in the 1940 Census*, Population Series P-3, No. 19, U. S. Department of Commerce, Washington, D. C., October 19, 1941, pp. 3-4.

In this situation the idea of more vocational education was advanced, not necessarily as a cure for unemployment, but as a factor which would offset to some extent the inexperience which handicapped youth when they sought jobs. This emphasis on education as a way out is not surprising; Americans have always believed in education and self-improvement as means of "getting ahead." And although the depression forced upon most people the realization that unemployment is a social and economic rather than an individual problem, popular faith in "practical education" as one way out did not disappear. Instead, the movement for expansion of our vocational training facilities gained new impetus during this period.

THE BACKGROUND OF VOCATIONAL TRAINING

The need for some means of perpetuating the skills of trained craftsmen is as old as civilization itself. Always there have been methods of training young workers to meet the needs of industry and commerce.

The roots of modern vocational education are to be found in the guild system of medieval Europe, which provided for long-term apprenticeship of children to master craftsmen. While the working and living conditions of apprentices in those days left much to be desired, the system usually resulted in the thorough training of young workers and their eventual attainment of the status of skilled craftsmen in numbers generally consistent with labor-market needs. With the Industrial Revolution and the rise of modern capitalism, however, the guilds began to decline. They were finally abolished at the end of the eighteenth century, after which time apprenticeship became optional and regulations for the training of workers were made much less rigid.[3]

Remnants of the old guilds, in the form of strict systems of apprenticeship, survived in certain industries under the sponsorship of employers and later of labor unions. By the middle of the nineteenth century, however, as the factory system expanded, so many new functions and occupations requiring skilled and semiskilled workers had made their appearance in the industrial process that some well-planned, highly integrated means of supplementing the skilled labor supply was clearly needed. In this situation many leaders of industry, labor, and education turned to the public schools. During the closing decades of the last century more and more of the European countries established far-reaching vocational school systems operated or regulated by the state.

[3] "Vocational Training: Problems and Trends," *International Labour Review*, Vol. XXXVII, No. 2, February 1938, p. 140.

In the United States the development of formal vocational training was retarded because the Industrial Revolution reached this country somewhat later than it reached Europe. As early as 1876 some persons became disturbed by the apparent superiority of European craftsmen over those trained in America, as demonstrated by the exhibits at the Philadelphia Centennial Exposition.[4] In spite of sentiment in this period for "practical" education, however, genuine vocational training made little headway for many years. Such courses as were introduced in the public schools in the last part of the nineteenth century were of the "industrial arts" type, such as manual training, rather than specialized preparation for specific vocations. These courses were based on the premise that training in the use of certain tools would enable a youth to learn how to use other tools more easily when he went to work. With the increasing complexity of our industrial economy, however, it soon became obvious that more specialized training—training for particular vocations—was needed, and a majority of educators began to favor training of the vocational type.

In 1906 the National Society for the Promotion of Industrial Education was formed, to work for legislation providing Federal aid to local vocational schools. This movement was supported by the National Education Association, as well as by the American Federation of Labor, which had always worked for free public education, and which saw in the new trend toward vocational training an opportunity to substitute free public schools for private vocational schools.

At the same time certain business organizations joined the fight for federally aided vocational training. As the need for skilled workers in industry became more and more acute, the National Association of Manufacturers, the National Metal Trades Association, and the United States Chamber of Commerce backed the plan of the National Society for the Promotion of Industrial Education. The combination of these business forces with those of the educators and trade unionists was powerful enough to create wide public discussion of the whole question of vocational education.

The time was most propitious for obtaining federally sponsored vocational training in the years just before and during the first World War. In 1914 Congress authorized the President to appoint a committee to investigate the whole question. The committee's report stressed the need for vocational education to prevent waste of labor power, to increase earnings, to supplement apprenticeship, to meet the increasing demand for trained workmen, and to democratize education. It also maintained that the sharpness of competition among nations for world trade made necessary the rapid building up of a highly skilled labor force:

---

[4] Russell, John Dale and Associates, *Vocational Education*, Staff Study No. 8, Advisory Committee on Education, Washington, D. C., 1938, p. 10.

The battles of the future between nations will be fought in the markets of the world. The nation will triumph . . . which is able to put the greatest amount of skill and brains into what it produces. Our foreign commerce, and to some extent our domestic commerce, are being threatened by the commercial prestige which Germany has won . . . France and England, and even far-off Japan, . . . are now establishing national systems of vocational education. In Germany, within the next few years, there will probably be no such thing as an untrained man. In the United States probably not more than 25,000 of the eleven or twelve million workers in manufacturing or mechanical pursuits have had an opportunity to acquire an adequate training for their work in life. . . .[5]

The report recommended that a system of vocational education be instituted in the public schools of less than college grade, with the States to share expenses with the Federal Government.

Another argument that was heard in many quarters was that the social unrest which prevailed at that time was due to a lack of economic independence among the working people, and would decrease if young people were able to get skilled work at higher wages. For example, one educator remarked that:

The nation must . . . recognize the social significance of vocational education . . . as a means of furthering the security of the established order. Undeniably, social unrest pervades the land. Everywhere one finds evidences of unsound conditions in the social fabric. They break out in the form of strikes and riots; in the demand for legislation regarding hours and conditions of work; in the propaganda of the socialist. . . . Vocational education . . . goes to the very root of the causes of the discontent. By providing a means for each man to find a way out and up it puts the divine spark of ambition in men.[6]

Perhaps the most important factor which helped to bring about Federal support of vocational training was the growing shortage of skilled labor which resulted from the preparedness program in the years 1916–1917. The shipyards and munitions industries were forced to develop their own supply of skilled laborers through hastily organized systems of apprenticeship. With this combination of circumstances, the proponents of Federal aid for vocational training were finally able in 1917 to persuade Congress to pass a bill incorporating most of the features recommended to the House of Representatives by the Commission on National Aid to Vocational Education in its report 3 years earlier.[7] The bill was signed by President Wilson on February 23, 1917.

The National Vocational Education Act (commonly known as the Smith-Hughes Act) was the first and most important of several laws

[5] *Report of the Commission on National Aid to Vocational Education, Together With Hearings on the Subject*, U. S. House of Representatives, 63d Cong., 2d sess., Doc. No. 1004, 1914, p. 23.

[6] Lapp, John A., "National Aid for Vocational Education," *Journal of Proceedings and Addresses*, National Education Association of the United States, Washington, D. C., 1915, pp. 322–333.

[7] See footnote 5 above.

providing for Federal support to secondary schools offering vocational training courses of specified types. The act provided continuing support on a rising scale, culminating in an appropriation of $7,167,000 in 1926 and every year thereafter. This sum was allocated among the States which accepted the provisions of the act and designated State boards for vocational education to cooperate with the Federal Board for Vocational Education. In line with the stated purpose of the act, that of promoting education in agriculture and the trades and industries (including home economics), these funds were to cover a maximum of 50 percent of the salaries of teachers in courses meeting Federal requirements in these fields, as well as part of the cost of the training of vocational teachers. Work was to be given not only in full-time day courses, but also in evening and extension classes to adults and youth who were already employed.[8] This act is still in operation and furnishes the basis for supplementary legislation providing for the further expansion of the federally aided system of vocational training.

Employers welcomed the new training system as a source of skilled labor during the war period. They demanded more and more training, many of them paying their employees while they were attending part-time trade schools. Vocational education under the Smith-Hughes Act expanded rapidly as a result of these conditions.

After the war was over the vocational schools continued to receive widespread support because of the small number of apprentices in the various skilled crafts. In 1922 it was estimated that only 1 apprentice was being trained for every 100 workers in the building trades, and only 1 for every 57 workers in all mechanical and manufacturing industries. (These figures included students in the day, evening, and continuation trade schools, as well as apprentices.)[9] Businessmen as well as educators therefore favored the expansion of the Smith-Hughes program. Enrollment in Smith-Hughes programs increased from 164,000 in 1918 to more than half a million in 1923 and more than a million in 1929. (See appendix table 1.)

As enrollment under the Smith-Hughes Act increased, as training in the public schools became more and more specialized, and as the vocational schools became more and more important as compared with the apprenticeship systems sponsored by the trade unions, organized labor began to show some opposition to certain aspects of the training system it had helped to sponsor many years before.

[8] 39 Stat. L. 929–936. See Russell and Associates, *op. cit.*, pp. 14 ff., for a concise summary of Federal legislation on vocational training and texts of the Smith-Hughes Act and subsequent acts.

[9] Filbey, Emery, "Vocational Education: an Economic Necessity," *Addresses and Proceedings*, National Education Association of the United States, Washington, D. C., 1922, pp. 1472–1480.

Several specific criticisms arose. In the first place, some labor unions resented the fact that instead of developing Smith-Hughes training programs for vocations which had no history of apprenticeship, such as auto-repair work, the early Smith-Hughes schools had entered fields where apprenticeship systems had long been established.[10] The unions objected to this policy on the grounds that it released partially trained workers to compete with craftsmen trained under the apprenticeship system, and tended to drive wages downward.

Labor organizations also charged that most vocational schools oriented their programs of instruction toward filling the needs of employers rather than toward augmenting the welfare of the organized workers in a trade. In 1935 the Metal Trades Department of the American Federation of Labor convention passed a resolution which said in part:

. . . tax funds have, in many instances, been given to schools located wholly within private industrial plants and operated in a manner which seriously affected wage earners, not only tending to overcrowd certain skilled trades, but in other ways to lower the prevailing wages in these skilled trades thereby increasing unemployment as well as lowering standards of living. . . .

Beginners are given a short course . . . and put to work . . . at wages much lower than those prevalent for that particular operation . . . while skilled workers in these crafts remain unemployed.

It is neither just nor reasonable that public funds should be used to maintain training schools for the exclusive benefit of a particular employer.

There are similar abuses in similar trades and industrial arts schools throughout the country.[11]

Another criticism of vocational training under the Smith-Hughes Act offered by labor organizations was that school authorities in many places failed to consider the labor point of view in planning and developing the content of vocational programs. As a result, said the unions, not enough attention was paid in the vocational schools to explaining the purposes and functions of labor unions and labor legislation.

Employers also criticized the vocational schools, chiefly for not turning out workers with well-developed skills in the trades and industries and for not providing training in many fields where trained workers were needed. Retail selling was often cited as an example of a field in which many youth found employment but for which training was not available in the Smith-Hughes schools.

In the years 1932–1934 enrollment decreased sharply in the trade and industrial programs, although it increased somewhat in the agricultural programs and held its own in the home economics

---

[10] Snedden, David A., "Whither Vocational Education?" *Occupations*, Vol. XV, No. 5, February 1937, pp. 389–394.

[11] American Federation of Labor, Metal Trades Department, *Proceedings of the Twenty-seventh Annual Convention*, Atlantic City, 1935, pp. 57–58, 79.

programs. This was a period marked by a general decline in the amount of Federal funds expended for vocational training, a decline due largely to the inability of certain communities to raise sufficient funds for matching the Federal money that was available under the Smith-Hughes Act and supplementary legislation.[12]

In 1929 the George-Reed Act had provided for a cumulative increase of $500,000 each year for Smith-Hughes training; and its successor, the George-Ellzey Act of 1934, provided $3,000,000 per year over and above the basic Smith-Hughes appropriation for the years 1935–1937.[13] As the expiration of the George-Ellzey Act approached, a new bill was prepared by the American Vocational Association to increase Federal support for vocational education. It was finally passed in slightly revised form and approved by President Roosevelt in June 1936. Known as the George-Deen Act, it took cognizance of the criticisms cited above and went a long way toward removing the basis for them. It more than doubled the Federal funds available each year for vocational training, temporarily eased the "matching" provision required of the States, prohibited the improper use of funds in private factories for "training apprentices," and extended the training programs to the distributive occupations (notably retail trade).[14] This act, like the Smith-Hughes Act, is still in effect.

THE CURRENT STATUS OF SMITH-HUGHES TRAINING

By 1939 there were some 1,200 public vocational schools in the United States (compared with about 29,000 "white-collar" high schools). In the year ending June 30, 1939, the Federal Government spent $19,433,000 for vocational training subsidies; and for every Federal dollar spent, State and local governments furnished $1.71 in order to maintain their vocational schools.[15]

In 1939 enrollment in federally aided vocational schools and classes passed the 2-million mark. It had doubled in the decade since 1929.

---

[12] Deffenbaugh, W. S., *Effects of the Depression Upon Public Elementary and Secondary Schools and Upon Colleges and Universities*, Bulletin, 1937, No. 2, Office of Education, U. S. Department of the Interior, Washington, D. C., 1938, p. 34.

[13] Russell and Associates, *op cit.*, pp. 18–19.

[14] 49 Stat. L. 1488–1490 (1936). See Russell and Associates, *op. cit.*, pp. 21 ff. Commercial courses have never been included under the Federal plan because existing secondary schools have provided ample training of this sort. The Federal subsidy has been reserved mainly for those programs requiring expensive shop equipment or technical instruction, and which would therefore have been taught adequately in only a few communities if Federal assistance had not been available.

[15] Lloyd, John H., "Expanding the Office of Education," *American Teacher*, Vol. XXIV, No. 8, April 1940, pp. 46–47. See also *Time*, Vol. XXXVI, Part 1, No. 1, July 8, 1940, p. 38.

Most of the increase, however, was in agriculture and home economics rather than in trade and industrial programs. (See appendix table 1.)

Of the 2 million persons in vocational schools in the school year 1938–39, just under half were in "all-day" (full-time) training programs. The full-time trainees, the group with which this study is primarily concerned, increased by about 17 percent from 1937–38 to 1938–39.

The 196,000 youth in full-time trade and industrial programs are of particular interest because of the reported shortages of skilled industrial labor in recent months. The number of youth enrolled in such programs showed a smaller increase than did the number in any other type of all-day program; but even so, it rose almost 7 percent from 1938 to 1939. (See appendix table 2.)

Besides the general trend toward expansion of vocational training shown in the above figures, there are several other significant recent and current trends in Smith-Hughes training in the secondary schools which should be noted. First is a reaction against the extreme specialization of training advocated a decade or more ago. An increasing number of authorities in this field have come to believe that since occupational needs and technological processes change rapidly, there should be more emphasis on general background material and less on detailed skills in the vocational schools, particularly in the early years of the training programs.[16]

There is also a trend toward the diversification of training in the larger urban centers, and toward the development of State or regional trade schools established to meet the needs of smaller communities which cannot afford separate vocational schools.[17] By these devices the vocational training system is able to meet needs of youth whom it had formerly failed to reach.

A third trend in recent years has been a gradual increase in the age of youth who enroll in full-time Smith-Hughes classes. Formerly many such youth were 14 to 16 years of age at entrance; today very few are under 16, and many are 18 years of age or over. This has been due partly to the fact that vocational schools in many cities select older youth, or even high-school graduates, whenever possible. Marked interest has also been shown recently in the development of technical vocational courses in junior colleges.[18]

[16] See *Education for American Life*, The Regents' Inquiry Into the Character and Cost of Public Education in the State of New York, New York: The McGraw-Hill Book Co., Inc., 1938, p. 22; and Russell and Associates, *op. cit.*, pp. 215–216.

[17] *Digest of Annual Reports of State Boards for Vocational Education to the U. S. Office of Education, Vocational Division, Fiscal Year Ended June 30, 1939*, U. S. Office of Education, Federal Security Agency, Washington, D. C., 1940, pp. 36–37.

[18] *Ibid.*, p. 36.

A final important trend in the development of secondary school vocational training programs has been an increasing emphasis upon cooperation with labor and employers in planning local programs and policies.[19]   This has helped to remove some of the causes of the criticism long directed by labor against the vocational training system.

Vocational training as it exists today in the public schools still leaves much to be desired, especially if it is assumed that every individual should have some sort of occupational training.[20]   A relatively small minority of urban high schools offer Smith-Hughes courses, and there are many lines of work for which no training is available in the public vocational schools.   Before extending the scope and changing the content of present-day training, however, it is necessary to find out to what extent our training system is successful and which types of training have been and are most productive of success in securing related employment, so that any expansion or development of vocational training may have the soundest possible basis.

VOCATIONAL TRAINING DURING THE DEFENSE PERIOD

It will be well, in passing, to describe briefly some of the special types of vocational training which have been developed to meet the short-term needs of the defense program.

Since the Battle of France, in May 1940, vocational training both for youth and for older workers has received great impetus.   During the first 18 months of the defense effort, through November 1941, nearly 2½ million persons enrolled for specialized training in order to qualify for jobs in defense industries.   Some 1,200 public vocational and trade schools, 155 colleges and universities, and 10,000 public school shops assisted with this program.   About 800,000 of these workers received supplementary training, in order to enable them to advance to more complex types of jobs than they were then holding; another 700,000 were in preemployment refresher courses, many of them displaced workers from nondefense industries; the National Youth Administration gave defense training to more than 400,000 youth; and still others were trained by the CCC, Army, Civil Aeronautics Authority, Maritime Commission, and other agencies.   Most of these training courses lasted only a few months—as little as 8 weeks in the case of some of the preemployment and supplementary training courses.

An additional 2 million persons, not included in the figures just quoted, had received in-plant training in defense factories, under

[19] *Ibid.*, pp. 9–10, 41.

[20] John Dale Russell expresses this point of view as follows: ". . . on practical as well as theoretical grounds, and from a social as well as from an individualistic point of view, it is necessary to equip every young person for some occupation so that he may contribute effectively to the satisfaction of human wants." (*Op. cit.*, p. 175.)

" . . . the defense program has given new impetus to training of the trade and industrial type."

arrangements made by employers with the OPM Labor Division, during the first year and a half of the emergency.

One source of information on the nature and results of short-term defense training is a monthly report of the Bureau of Employment Security, Social Security Board, on preemployment refresher training. For the first 11 months of 1941 the B. E. S. had data for 303,170 registrants in such courses. Of these, 53 percent were under 25 years of age, and 97 percent were white. Over 31 percent of the entire group were trained in machine-shop work, another 21 percent had courses in aviation services, and welding and sheet-metal work were next in order of frequency. The total number of workers leaving their training courses and the total number obtaining employment unfortunately are not known. But of 79,600 who were placed in jobs by or whose jobs were known to public employment offices, 87 percent obtained work utilizing their training. The proportion of skilled workers getting jobs utilizing their training was 95 percent; of semi-skilled workers, 94 percent; of unskilled workers, 64 percent; of clerical workers, 28 percent; and of service workers, only 5 percent.[21]

A somewhat more comprehensive report on preemployment refresher training, available in unpublished form at the United States Office of Education, shows that of approximately 250,000 persons whose pre-employment training was completed by June 30, 1941, about 145,000, or 58 percent, obtained employment; but the latter group contained some duplication, and included some jobs of very short duration. From these figures it may be estimated that not more than half of the unemployed persons who had completed short-term training courses had obtained jobs in their fields of training. These over-all results were not dissimilar to those obtained in the 1938 youth survey, described in the present report, in spite of the fact that the defense training courses were of much shorter duration than full-time Smith-Hughes training programs. Short-term supplementary and preemployment training had proved quite adequate to fill the needs of industry even in periods of extraordinary emergency as late as June 1941.

DESCRIPTION OF THE PRESENT STUDY

It was with a view to supplying needed information as to the results of secondary school vocational training, as shown by the work histories of trained youth, that the present study was undertaken. The Division of Social Research of the Works Progress Administration had initiated, in July 1938, a survey of some 30,000 young people in 7 representative cities in different sections of the country. Samples of

---

[21] Bureau of Employment Security, *Vocational Training Activities of Public Employment Offices, November 1941*, Social Security Board, Washington, D. C., 1941, Table J–5.

youth who graduated from the eighth grade in the years 1929, 1931, and 1933 were selected so that youth of different ages, who had entered the labor market at different periods of the depression, could be studied. The principal results of this larger survey, in terms of the employment status of youth and their experiences since leaving school, are embodied in several reports of the Division of Research.[22]

While this survey of youth in the labor market was being conducted, local authorities in several cities expressed great interest in seeing any data which would cast light upon the effectiveness of vocational training. The youth survey provided an unusual opportunity to study the results of vocational training in terms of employment, since it covered both the training and the subsequent work histories of youth. This aspect of the larger survey was therefore singled out for special study.

Because of difficulties in arriving at a uniform definition of what constitutes vocational training, the present analysis of the results of such training is for the most part limited to youth who had entered full-time day training programs in the federally aided vocational high-school system. The Smith-Hughes Act had established certain basic standards: namely, uniform courses of study, methods of instruction, and minimum qualifications of teachers; a school year continuing for at least 9 months; and instruction covering at least 30 hours per week, with half of the attendance time devoted to practical work. By studying the results of training acquired under these regulations, it was possible to draw conclusions more widely applicable than would have been the case if other less standardized types of occupational training had been included.

In three of the seven cities in which the survey of youth in the labor market was carried on, vocational instruction under the Smith-Hughes Act was not offered during all or part of the period studied.

---

[22] The first of these, entitled *Urban Youth: Their Characteristics and Economic Problems*, was a preliminary report on the status of youth on July 1, 1938, based on field tallies in the seven cities. (Series I, No. 24, Division of Research, Works Progress Administration, Washington, D. C., 1939.) A second report, *Disadvantaged Youth on the Labor Market*, by Stanley L. Payne, was a brief account of the characteristics and labor-market activities of youth in the seven cities who had been victims of long-time unemployment. (Series I, No. 25, Division of Research, Work Projects Administration, Federal Works Agency, 1940.) *Thirty Thousand Urban Youth*, also by Stanley L. Payne, is a brief, nontechnical summary of the results of the youth survey. (Social Problems Series No. 6, Work Projects Administration, Federal Works Agency, Washington, D. C., 1940.) A fourth report, *Getting Started: Urban Youth in the Labor Market*, by Albert Westefeld, is a more detailed analysis of the experiences of youth in the labor market throughout the depression. (Monograph No. XXVI, Division of Research, Work Projects Administration, Federal Works Agency, Washington, D. C., 1942, in preparation.)

The study of vocational training in relation to employment was therefore limited to the remaining four cities—St. Louis, Birmingham, Denver, and Seattle.

The number of vocationally trained youth in the original survey sample (which included on the average less than half of the youth in the eighth-grade classes of 1929, 1931, and 1933) was too small to permit detailed analysis of many individual training programs. The sample of vocationally trained youth was therefore enlarged to include all youth of the three eighth-grade classes studied who had been enrolled in a full-time Smith-Hughes training program for one semester or more. In addition, youth with full-time commercial training in the vocational schools were interviewed, although this training was not financed with the help of Smith-Hughes funds. Under this definition the total number of vocationally trained youth who were interviewed was just over 3,000, with more than 2,400 of these in St. Louis alone. Because of the large number of trained youth in St. Louis, much of the detailed analysis of specific training programs and their results had to be confined to that city.

In the following report chapter I consists of a general discussion of the problems involved in any evaluation of vocational training. Chapter II includes a brief analysis of the background and characteristics of vocationally trained youth as contrasted with other youth, and describes the types of training they acquired. Chapter III presents a comparison of trained and untrained youth in terms of economic status. Chapter IV is an analysis of the relationship of selected types of training which youth had undergone and their success in getting the kinds of work for which they were trained. Chapter V includes a study of employment in relation to vocational training in the regular high schools of Seattle as compared with the Smith-Hughes school in that city and a discussion of the comparative success in the labor market of youth who had been trained in private vocational schools in all four cities and those who had received Smith-Hughes training in the public vocational schools. Chapter VI describes the experiences of trained youth with regard to vocational guidance and placement and their attitudes toward vocational training. The concluding chapter is a discussion of some of the questions commonly raised about vocational training, presented in the light of the data supplied by the present survey.

SUMMARY

THE PURPOSE of the present study is to supply information regarding the characteristics and work histories of youth who have received full-time vocational training under the standards established by the Smith-Hughes Act. The data presented below are based mainly on interviews with 3,042 such youth in St. Louis, Birmingham, Denver, and Seattle. Comparisons were also made between Smith-Hughes trained youth and other youth who were interviewed in the same cities in connection with the more comprehensive survey of youth in the labor market.

CHARACTERISTICS AND TRAINING OF THE YOUTH

In spite of the prevalent belief that vocational school students as a group come from poor social backgrounds, the data gathered indicated that they did not differ significantly in this respect from youth who did not attend vocational school in the four cities where the survey was conducted. Family occupational backgrounds and social status, as measured by average rental values in the districts where the youth lived, were much the same in the trained and untrained groups. Nor were the trained youth markedly different from other youth in scholastic ability, as measured by age at eighth-grade graduation.

In years of education completed, however, Smith-Hughes trained youth in the four cities were clustered more closely about the average for all youth than were those without Smith-Hughes training. Fewer of the trained than of the untrained youth had dropped out of school at an early age, and only a sixth as many had gone on to college. On the average, trained youth were only 3 or 4 months behind untrained youth in total amount of schooling completed.

A majority of the trained youth interviewed had been registered in commercial programs operating under Smith-Hughes standards. Youth trained in the trades and industries were second, followed by girls with training in "women's programs" such as home economics, power sewing, and beauty culture or cosmetology. Students trained in the arts programs were fewer in number.

There was a slight tendency for youth to acquire training in the same general occupational fields as those in which their fathers usually worked. The sons and daughters of clerical workers went into the accounting and secretarial programs, for example, and the sons of semiskilled workers into the machine-shop program, in a higher proportion of cases than would have been expected on a basis of chance. But the youth did not follow very closely in their parents' footsteps.

Only a little over a third of all trained youth had completed their training. Students of cosmetology and the more specialized commercial subjects completed their programs in the highest proportion of cases. Those who dropped out gave "preference for work" and "lack of funds" as their reasons for not completing their training in most cases.

EMPLOYMENT AND EARNINGS OF TRAINED YOUTH

More than nine-tenths of all trained youth had entered the labor market at some time, and more than four-fifths were still working or seeking work at the time of interview. The proportion of all trained youth who were employed increased fairly steadily until 1937, when a business recession caused a slight drop in employment. At the time of interview, as of July 1, 1938, 82 out of every 100 trained youth in the labor market had jobs, 75 of them in full-time work. The highest proportion of employment was found among older, white, male youth, and (except in St. Louis) youth with completed training. In each city except Seattle, trained youth had slightly more employment than did untrained youth. This advantage was most apparent among young men.

When the factor of amount of education was taken into account in the trained and untrained groups, it was found that labor-market experience was worth about as much as an equal period of Smith-Hughes training, as far as assistance in getting jobs was concerned.

The average earnings of trained youth at the time of interview ranged from $16 per week in St. Louis to $18.90 in Denver (where only male youth were included in the group studied). There was no consistent difference in earnings between the trained and untrained groups as such. Young women had progressively higher earnings as their period of Smith-Hughes training increased in length; but among young men there was no indication that Smith-Hughes training paid dividends in increased earning power.

As the trained youth grow older their position in the labor market may compare more favorably with that of untrained youth. All indications from the present survey are, however, that future differences between trained and untrained youth, in terms of employment and wage status, are likely to be very small.

EMPLOYMENT IN RELATION TO SPECIFIC TYPES OF TRAINING

In all but a few instances, the various types of training showed at least a tendency to lead to employment of a related sort. In general, trained youth were more likely to go into clerical, skilled, and semi-skilled work, and less likely to enter professional, managerial, and unskilled work, than were untrained youth. Commercially trained youth went into clerical types of work in a higher proportion of cases than industrially trained youth went into skilled or semiskilled work.

About three-fifths of all trained youth had at some time had jobs with some degree of relationship to their training, in each city except Denver. More young women than young men had worked at jobs in which their training was of some value to them. About three-fourths of all youth with completed training had obtained related employment, compared with only about half of the youth who did not complete their training programs.

There were wide differences among the various programs in terms of the proportion of trainees who obtained related employment. This was due not only to the quality of the training received and the state of the labor market, but also to the breadth of the different fields for which youth were trained. In spite of the prevalent idea that the schools are training too many youth in commercial courses, commercial students, particularly those from the more specialized programs, proved better able to get related jobs after they left vocational school than did youth with other kinds of training. In St. Louis almost two-thirds of the commercially trained youth, compared with a little over half of the youth with training in the trades and industries and in women's programs, had held jobs with some relationship to their training. The proportion of youth who had had jobs directly related to their training ranged from 83 percent of the girls trained in the cosmetology program down to 14 percent of the young men trained in sheet-metal work.

A month-by-month analysis of the employment status of trained youth over the period 1930–1938 showed that the proportions employed in their fields of training increased fairly steadily, particularly in times of rising business activity. The increase, which was especially large among young women who had left the eighth grade in 1929, was apparently due to the cumulative effect of training, to increasing maturity and experience, and to the generally rising level of employment after 1933 which gave the youth more chance to choose their jobs.

Both the first jobs and the jobs held at time of interview by those who had completed their training were twice as likely to be directly related to the training received as were the jobs of those with uncompleted training. In St. Louis students with completed training in the cosmetology, machine-shop, and special commercial programs were most likely to go into directly related work. Youth with completed training had jobs of longer average duration than other youth; but there was no consistent relationship between completion of training and earnings.

Young men trained in the trades and industries and youth of both sexes trained in the arts received the highest earnings of all groups of trained youth studied in St. Louis. The range of earnings on all full-time jobs was from an average of $17.40 per week for former students of drafting down to an average of $10.60 for former cosmetology students. In general, youth trained in women's and commercial programs (principally girls) received the lowest earnings.

It is significant that youth trained in some of the programs which had the best records for placements on related jobs worked long hours, had below-average earnings, and showed little increase in earnings from first job to job held at time of interview. Girls trained in cosmetology were an outstanding example of this. At the other extreme, young men trained in several programs with low records of placement in related fields, such as woodwork and sheet-metal work, earned about as much as the average industrially trained youth.

VOCATIONAL TRAINING OUTSIDE THE SMITH-HUGHES SYSTEM

Is vocational training under the Smith-Hughes system superior to training in the regular high schools and the private vocational schools? To get at the answer to this question, data were obtained concerning training of a vocational type in regular high-school classes (those not under Smith-Hughes standards) in one city. Some data on the labor-market status of youth trained in private vocational schools were also gathered in all four cities.

Seattle was the only city where it was possible roughly to compare the results of Smith-Hughes training with those of other types of training. Youth who had completed certain minimum requirements in regular high-school vocational courses there were classed as vocationally trained; and these youth were better off than Smith-Hughes trained youth in Seattle, both with respect to the proportion having employment and in terms of the average wages they drew. They reported less employment that was related to their training, however, than did youth with Smith-Hughes training at Seattle's Edison Vocational School. When the Smith-Hughes group was divided into persons with completed and uncompleted training, the regular high-school trainees fell in between these two groups as far as success in obtaining related employment was concerned.

A wide variety of private vocational schools were available to youth in all four cities. On the whole, these schools apparently enabled their students to get jobs more readily than youth trained in the Smith-Hughes schools. The earnings of private vocational school graduates, however, were no higher than those of youth in the four cities who had received no training at all. Private vocational schools tend to attract older, more mature, and more experienced students than do the public schools. This may account in part for the high proportion of their graduates who found employment.

GUIDANCE, PLACEMENT, AND ATTITUDES OF TRAINED YOUTH

Only one-sixth of the trained youth who were interviewed reported having received at school any occupational guidance which led to their entering Smith-Hughes training programs. In spite of widespread discussion of the need for guidance, in each of the four cities studied there was too little personnel available to permit extensive individual counseling. A large majority of youth decided upon their vocations through the inexpert advice of parents or friends, or because of various chance factors.

Over half of all trained youth reported that their vocational training had helped them in getting jobs, and three-fifths said that their school work had been of assistance to them in working on the job. These figures were very similar to those obtained from the analysis of the actual work histories of the youth. Those who were employed full time at the date of interview, those who had completed their training programs, girls, white youth, and youth with commercial training all attributed to their vocational training more than an average amount of assistance in getting jobs.

Of every 20 youth, 19 believed that vocational training should be expanded in the public schools. A supplementary questionnaire in Seattle showed that almost as high a proportion of youth outside the Smith-Hughes school and of the parents of all youth held the same belief.

When asked if they had any criticisms of the vocational training they had undergone, half of the youth simply said, "It was worth while." The most common specific criticism, particularly among youth with completed training, was that the programs offered in Smith-Hughes schools were incomplete.

Only 8 trained youth in every 100 reported that they had located 1 job or more through the schools, and another 6 said that they had found work through public or private employment agencies. While these ratios were twice as high as those which obtained among other youth, they showed that only a small minority of the youth had been able to find work through the schools or placement agencies.

When questioned as to their plans for the future, more than three-fifths of the trained youth showed their preoccupation with economic problems by stating that they hoped to secure employment, retain or advance in their present jobs, or get better jobs.

CONCLUSIONS

The results of the present study indicate that there is a need for more adequate vocational guidance for youth, to make possible the selection of those who are best qualified for training. In addition, the instruction and equipment used in training programs should be the sort best calculated to prepare youth for actual conditions on the job. Specialization of training should be encouraged in fields where no system of apprenticeship exists, and in other fields the content of the training programs should be worked out cooperatively by the schools and the agencies sponsoring apprentices.

The wide differences among youth with various types of training, as far as their experiences in the labor market were concerned, suggest that the utmost care should be taken to adjust vocational training to labor-market needs of the present and the immediate future. This applies both to the number of youth trained and to the types of training offered. If such an adjustment is not achieved, the skills of trained youth may be lost through inability to get jobs of the sort for which they are trained.

Placement facilities for youth should be expanded, in order to minimize unemployment and to place youth in employment in fields related to training. Finally, on the basis of the experiences of placement agencies and of constant research into labor-market needs, vocational educators should continually readjust their methods and their curricula so as to meet the changing needs of our modern industrial economy.

Chapter I

VOCATIONAL TRAINING: THE PROBLEMS INVOLVED

PUBLIC SCHOOL vocational training of a specialized type is a comparatively recent development in this country. Within the space of a single generation it has evolved from rudimentary "manual training" to an extensive and well-organized system with some 2 million students registered in federally aided Smith-Hughes vocational schools alone in 1939.

Because of its newness and the rapidity of its growth, vocational training is still a highly controversial subject. It means many things to many people. To the educator it means an opportunity to round out the school curriculum with practical training of a sort that appeals to certain types of youth; to the employer it means a source of trained labor; and to the trade unionist it means on the one hand a valuable means of obtaining free supplementary training, and on the other a competitor of the apprenticeship system which may produce an oversupply of trained or partly trained workers to compete with skilled craftsmen in certain fields. These points of view meet in a common desire for free public school training which would produce efficient skilled or semiskilled workers in fields where apprenticeship training facilities are inadequate to meet labor-market needs.

Most of the issues which arise in discussing and attempting to evaluate vocational education may be reduced to a few fundamental problems. Some of these are discussed briefly below.[1] The results of the present survey of vocational training in four cities have considerable bearing on these questions.

---

[1] For a more detailed treatment of the issues involved in vocational training see Russell, John Dale and Associates, *Vocational Education*, Staff Study Number 8, Advisory Committee on Education, Washington, D. C., 1938; and Norton, Thomas L., *Education for Work*, The Regents' Inquiry Into the Character and Cost of Public Education in the State of New York, New York: The McGraw-Hill Book Co., Inc., 1938.

SELECTION OF STUDENTS FOR TRAINING

If vocational training is to attain a maximum of efficiency, students with some aptitude for and interest in the work must be selected for the various training programs. From the days when industrial arts and manual training courses were first installed in our public schools, however, it has been a common practice in many places to send youth who could not make passing grades in academic work into vocational classes. This was done on the theory that if a youth cannot learn to use his brain effectively, at least he can learn to use his hands so as to become a self-supporting member of society. The result has often been that the brightest students have entered college preparatory courses, and the next brightest commercial courses, while "industrial courses were given to pupils who were not able to pass any of the other courses regardless of their aptitude for industrial work." [2] Several studies have shown students in vocational schools to be lower in scholastic aptitudes than students in regular high schools. [3] There is little evidence that this was a serious problem, however, in the four cities covered by the present study.

In some places an attempt is being made to overcome the tendency to consider vocational training as being primarily for dull students. In New York State only the more capable students are encouraged to apply for training in the skilled trades. [4] Another example of a restrictive policy is to be found at the Thomas A. Edison Vocational School in Seattle. The forerunner of this school, the Broadway Opportunity School, was attended mainly by students of low scholastic achievement. Gradually, however, standards were raised until by 1938 a rigid selection of students was being made by the Edison school, and a majority of its full-time day students were high-school graduates. Under this policy the level of vocational training is raised; but youth who cannot qualify for trade programs are forced to take commercial courses or no vocational work at all.

If it be admitted that vocational training is most valuable when it is given to youth who are best equipped by ability and temperament to profit by it, selection of candidates for such training is necessary, even though some less able youth are excluded from the vocational schools. This implies an efficient system of vocational guidance to gauge the abilities of youth and to counsel them regarding opportunities in the various fields of work to which they are attracted.

[2] Eckert, Ruth E. and Marshall, Thomas O., *When Youth Leave School*, The Regents' Inquiry Into the Character and Cost of Public Education in the State of New York, New York: The McGraw-Hill Book Co., Inc., 1938, p. 314.

[3] Norton, *op. cit.*, p. 65.

[4] *Ibid.*, pp. 60–61.

Various studies indicate, however, that only a minority of students receive any vocational guidance at all.[5]

THE CONTENT OF VOCATIONAL INSTRUCTION

A debate has long been raging over the question of general versus specific types of vocational instruction. Should our vocational schools try to turn out finished craftsmen? Or should courses on the secondary school level be limited to giving a general background of information about a group of related courses, leaving the acquisition of manipulative skills until the youth is further advanced, either in school or on the job?

Proponents of the former policy, mainly employers, argue that vocational training is of little practical benefit unless it enables youth to go directly into skilled employment. Their opponents, chiefly labor groups, claim that youth cannot learn real skills under classroom conditions, but only on the job. The secondary school, they say, should give the youth a chance to study and sample various types of work open to him; and once he has made a tentative choice of occupations, it should give him a general social and economic background in his field—a phase of training which has often been neglected. He should also become acquainted with labor and social legislation which may affect him when he goes to work. Under such a system, in the last year or two of his vocational program he would be taught certain basic skills which would aid him in getting his first job. The more difficult skills would be learned either on the job or in an advanced training course extending beyond the secondary school level.[6]

These two viewpoints can, of course, be reconciled. In trades where an apprenticeship system exists, the schools can cooperate with the employers or unions sponsoring such a system. As long as it operates efficiently in supplying the labor-market need for skilled workers, the schools could give only general background or supplementary training to help in turning out well-educated, expert workers. This is desirable because it means a closer coordination of training with labor-market needs, and because physical skills can best be learned by actual practice on the job.

In fields where no adequate system of apprenticeship is in operation, specialization of training is necessary for best results. This is particularly

---

[5] For example, of 13,000 Maryland youth interviewed in 1936, less than a fourth of all youth (less than a third of all urban youth) had received vocational guidance. (Bell, Howard M., *Youth Tell Their Story*, American Council on Education, American Youth Commission, Washington, D. C., 1938, p. 74.)

[6] See *Education for American Life*, The Regents' Inquiry Into the Character and Cost of Public Education in the State of New York, New York: The McGraw-Hill Book Co., Inc., 1938, p. 22.

true outside the industrial training fields, where there are no apprentice-ship systems. General training should not be neglected, however, in any case. A background of general knowledge and scientific theory should be a part of every trained youth's schooling, in order to lay the groundwork for the acquisition of new skills on the job. If this aspect of training is neglected, the trained worker will be less able to adapt himself to changing economic and technological conditions.

It should be recognized that training in vocational school probably will never be able to replace actual experience on the job in turning out skilled industrial workers with well-rounded practical training. There are several reasons for this. First, conditions in the school shop will never be the same as conditions in the workshop or factory; the school, with its limited finances, can hardly hope to equal the variety of processes and the complexity of machinery used on the job. Second, the youth in vocational school is younger and less experienced than the average young worker. He must also be protected from certain of the dangers which exist on the job, for an accident in the vocational school shop might reflect discredit on the school. In some trades, such as machine shop, the scope of his training is therefore limited to the simplest and least dangerous types of work.

The present study casts some light on this whole issue by evaluating the results of various sorts of training. The results of general and specialized training, as well as of the different programs and types of programs, will be compared whenever possible.

VOCATIONAL TRAINING IN RELATION TO LABOR-MARKET NEEDS

The number of trained youth turned out by a particular program should correspond closely to the number of job openings in that field, if labor-market needs are to be met and if at the same time all trained youth are to have at least a good chance of getting employment that is related to their vocational school work. Complaints from employers and from labor indicate that the vocational schools frequently fail to regulate the number of youth trained so as to bring about this close relationship.

In one conference of educators, employers, and labor unionists, for instance, employers of labor in the needle trades and in the printing industry claimed that they needed more skilled labor. Union repre-sentatives maintained, on the other hand, that many skilled clothing workers were unemployed, and that in the printing industry sufficient apprentices were being trained to meet labor-market needs.[7] In one of the cities covered by the present survey the auto mechanics' union complained in 1938 that the local Smith-Hughes school was training

---

[7] "Integration of Occupational Training and Employment" (Report of Confer-ence on Employment and Guidance, Welfare Council of New York City, Novem-ber 19, 1937), *Occupations*, January 1938, pp. 340–345.

". . . a background of general knowledge . . . to lay the groundwork for the acquisition of new skills . . ."

too many auto mechanics, who entered the labor market with little practical experience and took low-paid jobs at a time when many skilled union members were unemployed.

In part this sort of conflict is unavoidable. Employers and labor representatives are nearly always in disagreement as to the number of new workers needed at a given time. Furthermore, the need for labor fluctuates, so it is usually impossible to tell more than a few months ahead how many workers will be able to find jobs. For example, in 1938 and 1939 there were tens of thousands of unemployed machinists, toolmakers, and diemakers; but in 1940 the supply of highly skilled workers in these fields was running very low.

There seems no doubt that expansion of public school vocational training is desirable in fields where no adequate apprenticeship training is available or where there is a shortage of trained workers. It would be particularly useful in lines of work for which there has been, until recently at least, no formal training. For example, in the field of domestic service, standardized training, such as that given on Work Projects Administration and National Youth Administration training projects, tends to raise the efficiency and earning power of the workers. Expansion of training for many types of skilled jobs in the defense industries was also necessary in 1940 and 1941.

The extension of vocational training beyond the high-school level is certainly desirable in order that mature, highly skilled technical workers may be turned out. Several educational surveys have recommended that provisions be made for giving advanced vocational training at the thirteenth and fourteenth grade levels in technical institutes or postgraduate courses, to train technical assistants and highly skilled workers.[8] Such a plan would provide valuable training on a higher level than is now available in Smith-Hughes vocational schools, in such fields as laboratory research.

The public vocational schools still reach a comparatively small minority of youth. In 1930 only about 8 percent of the high schools in urban centers offered vocational training in trades and industries under the Smith-Hughes plan. Today the proportion is somewhat larger, especially since the defense program has given new impetus to training of the trade and industrial type. The New York Regents' Inquiry maintains, however, that vocational adjustment should be the schools' responsibility to all youth, and that democratic education must give every child "the opportunity to pursue that type of education which will best advance his own welfare in ways consistent with the welfare of society."[9] Such a policy would entail the expansion

[8] Norton, *op. cit.*, p. 142. See also *A Survey of the Common School System of Washington*, Washington State Planning Council, Olympia, Sept. 24, 1938, p. 56.

[9] Norton, *op. cit.*, p. 141.

of training facilities in the schools on the basis of long-range planning rather than one of immediate needs, and also considerable revision of the curricula of vocational and other secondary schools.

The schools have a responsibility to the employers to supplement the labor supply with skilled workers where they are needed; a responsibility to labor not to flood the labor market with too great a supply of partly skilled workers and thereby drive wages down; and a responsibility to the students not to turn out trained youth in such numbers that many cannot find jobs, with the result that they lose their skills and their morale suffers. Whether these three obligations can be reconciled by a process of planning the training programs in cooperation with labor and industry and providing for rapid expansion of training facilities when new needs arise, is a problem of major importance in the vocational field.

VOCATIONAL PLACEMENT

The training of youth for useful occupations is only a part of the problem of vocational adjustment. It must be preceded by effective vocational guidance and followed by efficient placement to insure that knowledge and skill, once acquired, will be used.

The placement of youth is a more difficult problem than the placement of more mature workers, because many youth have had no specialized training or work experience. For this reason specialized placement agencies catering to the youth group are desirable—agencies which can offer youth advice and counsel as well as opportunities for placement. In the last few years junior placement services embodying these functions have greatly increased in number. Three principal agencies have participated separately or in cooperation with one another in the extension of junior placement facilities: the United States Employment Service, the National Youth Administration, and the public schools. In addition to public placement agencies open to all youth, most vocational schools take some responsibility for the placement of their graduates.

Many cities, however, still have no special placement offices for youth. Where such offices exist many unemployed youth do not take advantage of them, and only a minority of those who do apply are successfully placed on permanent jobs. This failure of junior placement offices to serve a majority of youth may be attributable in individual cases to depressed labor-market conditions, lack of guidance and training prior to application for employment, inadequately staffed placement offices, lack of cooperation between schools and public employment services, or any combination of these factors.

RESEARCH IN THE VOCATIONAL FIELD

An efficient system of vocational adjustment depends in large part on the development of an adequate research program. Some research on occupational trends has been done by Federal agencies, but for the most part it has remained for private organizations to popularize this research and to make the current facts about vocational opportunities available to the educator and the youth in need of guidance.[10] A few local communities have made surveys of job opportunities for youth, but the technique of such surveys is rudimentary as yet.

Follow-up studies to assess the actual value of vocational training are almost completely lacking. Many vocational schools keep records of the number of their graduates who obtain first jobs, but few schools check on them again once they have been placed. Several schools and school boards have made cursory surveys of employment and unemployment among youth.[11] But for the most part these have been limited to high-school graduates, ignoring students who have dropped out. Some of these surveys have been based on mail questionnaires, with only partial returns; and as a rule they have been aimed only at determining the general situation as to employment and unemployment, without regard to vocational training.

In only a few cases have local surveys attempted to compare youth with vocational training in the public schools with other young people as to employment and earnings. In 1937 the Regents' Inquiry surveyed 1,641 graduates of regular high schools in New York State and 324 graduates of specialized vocational schools, all of whom had graduated from 6 to 11 months before. It was found that only 11 percent of the male vocational school graduates were jobless, compared with 26 percent of the boys without training. Corresponding figures for the girl graduates were 37 and 46 percent. The boy vocational school graduates earned an average of $18.50 per week, compared with $14.63 for the boy graduates of regular high schools. About 63 percent of the boy vocational school graduates and 79 percent of the girl graduates who were employed were working at the types of jobs for which they had been trained. A third of the boy graduates and two-thirds of the boy withdrawals from vocational schools said that they were not even partly trained for the jobs they held.[12]

[10] See, for example, the magazines *Occupations* and *Vocational Trends;* also *Occupational Outlines of America's Major Occupations,* 1940, and the series of occupational monographs published by Science Research Associates, Chicago, Ill.

[11] See particularly studies made by school authorities in Baltimore, Md.; Minneapolis, Minn.; Milwaukee, Wis.; Denver, Colo.; and Springfield, Mo.; also Jessen, Carl A.; and Hutchins, H. Clifton, *Youth: Community Surveys,* Bulletin No. 18–VI, U. S. Office of Education, U. S. Department of the Interior, Washington, D. C., 1936.

[12] Norton, *op. cit.,* pp. 16–24.

Another study, made in Philadelphia, disclosed that less than two-thirds of the graduates from trade and industrial courses were working in occupations related to their training.[13]   A survey made in Essex County, N. J., in 1935 indicated that of the trained white youth 16 to 24 years of age who had jobs, two-thirds of the girls but less than half of the boys were working in occupations for which they were trained.[14]

A survey of working youth under 18 years of age in six States, made by the Children's Bureau of the United States Department of Labor in 1936, showed a still smaller proportion of employment in field of training on the last jobs of vocationally trained youth.   Only 19 percent of the young trained workers 16 and 17 years of age, and 8 percent of those under 16, were working at jobs in which they used their training.   Of the 16- and 17-year-old workers who had had some training but had failed to complete any definite course, only 13 percent were employed on jobs related to their training, compared with 43 percent of those who had completed their training.[15]   But the fact that this group consisted only of youth under 18 makes it hardly comparable with the group studied in the present survey, which comprised for the most part young workers 18 to 24 years of age.

Very little has been done either by private or by Federal agencies, however, to determine the results of specific vocational training programs in terms of actual employment.   According to the report of the Advisory Committee on Education:

Research of an evaluative type has been very limited in the Federal program of vocational education, and yet this type of research is a fundamental necessity to sound development. . . .   Little or no evidence has been gathered regarding the results or effectiveness of the instruction given.[16]

In order to aid in the planning of vocational training programs, frequent surveys should be made, not only to measure trends in employment in various localities and regions, but also to determine the relative success of graduates from each program in obtaining jobs

---

[13] Pavan, Ann, "A Follow-up Study of Philadelphia Public School Graduates, 1935," *Occupations*, Vol. XVI, No. 3, December 1937, pp. 252–259.   See also *How Fare Philadelphia Public School Graduates*, Junior Employment Service of the School District of Philadelphia, Pennsylvania State Employment Service, affiliated with U. S. Employment Service, Philadelphia, Pa., February 1939.

[14] *Coming of Age in Essex County*, Essex County Superintendent of Schools and University of Newark Research Center, Newark, N. J., 1939, pp. 16–20, 31–32.

[15] Wood, Helen, *Young Workers and Their Jobs in 1936: A Survey in Six States*, Publication No. 249, U. S. Department of Labor, Children's Bureau, Washington, D. C., 1940, p. 25.

[16] Russel, *op. cit.*, p. 49.

related to their training. An annual survey of employment opportunities and of the employment status of trained youth by school authorities in each community where Smith-Hughes training is offered would help to provide the information necessary for evaluating the various programs and for planning their expansion or contraction, locally and nationally.

Chapter II

CHARACTERISTICS AND TRAINING
OF THE YOUTH

BEFORE ATTEMPTING to evaluate the results of Smith-Hughes vocational training in terms of employment and earnings, it is necessary to discuss briefly the characteristics of the youth who received training and the types of training they received.

CHARACTERISTICS OF TRAINED YOUTH

The characteristics of youth may be conveniently divided into four categories: their social and economic backgrounds, their scholastic abilities, the education they have completed, and their sex and racial composition as a group. The present study showed practically no difference in social-economic status between Smith-Hughes trained youth and other or "untrained" youth;[1] nor were there any significant differences between trained and untrained youth in scholastic ability, except possibly in Birmingham. A comparison of the two groups as to sex and race showed some differences, however. The trained group showed a marked preponderance of girls (in St. Louis and Seattle), and an underrepresentation of Negroes. Apparently such selection as had occurred was based mainly on sex and race, rather than on social backgrounds and abilities.

---

[1] Unless otherwise specified, the terms "vocationally trained" and "Smith-Hughes trained" are used interchangeably throughout this report to signify youth with one semester or more of full-time training under Smith-Hughes standards, whether or not that training was actually financed by Smith-Hughes funds, and whether or not it was completed. "Untrained," unless otherwise specified, means those without as much as one semester of Smith-Hughes type training, although "untrained" youth may have had courses of a vocational nature in regular high schools or in private schools.

Social and Economic Backgrounds

There were no important differences between the youth with and without Smith-Hughes training as far as their parents' occupations were concerned. Half of both the trained youth and the untrained youth in St. Louis said that their fathers were skilled or semiskilled workers.[2] The only consistent difference between the two groups was that the trained youth were a little more likely than the untrained youth to have fathers who were skilled workers. This was true in each of the four cities. (See appendix table 3.)

The youth who took vocational training came from poorer homes than the average in Denver and Seattle; but in the other two cities fewer Smith-Hughes trained youth came from low-rental areas, and more from medium-rental areas, than was true of youth as a whole.[3] (See appendix table 4.)

Scholastic Ability

There was no statistically reliable evidence that the trained youth were markedly inferior as students to the other youth. One measure of scholastic ability is age at the time of eighth-grade graduation. By this criterion trained youth were approximately equal to untrained youth in average [4] age in three of the four cities. The only notable variation was in Birmingham, where trained youth were on the average 6 months older than other youth when they completed grade school. (See appendix table 5.) This difference might have been accentuated if Negro youth had been eliminated from the untrained group, to render it more fully comparable with the trained group, since Smith-Hughes training was not available to Negro youth in Birmingham.

Another check on school aptitudes, available only in Birmingham, was a tabulation of the results of the 10 Stanford Achievement Tests. This showed that vocationally trained youth in that city were about equal in average scholastic achievement to other youth of the same ages. But when the trained and untrained groups were made comparable by the elimination of the Negroes from the untrained group, there was

[2] In determining the father's occupational classification, the occupation followed longest during the previous 10 years was chosen. There was probably a tendency on the part of the youth to report a higher percentage of fathers' jobs as being in the occupations with the greatest amount of prestige, and a lower percentage in semiskilled and unskilled occupations, than was actually the case.

[3] Low-rental areas were defined as those inhabited by approximately the bottom 25 percent of all youth (in terms of average rentals paid by their families). The medium-rental group included roughly the middle 50 percent, and the high-rental group the top 25 percent, of all youth in terms of the rent paid by their parents.

[4] Unless otherwise specified, the term "average" refers to the median throughout this report when data gathered in the present survey are under consideration.

a significant difference between the two groups. All white youth in Birmingham had an average score of 8.72 on the battery of tests, compared with 8.13 for the trained (white) youth only, on a scale where 8.8 (representing the eighth month of the eighth school grade) was the expected average. The principal difference between the trained and untrained groups lay in the range of scores rather than in the averages. The trained youth seemed to be clustered more closely about the average, with fewer very bright or very dull students, than the untrained youth.[5]

Although there seems to have been at one time a tendency to send Birmingham youth of comparatively poor abilities to vocational school, this seems largely to have been corrected. According to one youth trained as an auto mechanic in that city:

> In the 2 years I was at Paul Hayne, the school had the reputation of being a catchall for misfits—boys who couldn't make the grade in regular academic classes or who couldn't adjust to high-school discipline. But the auto mechanics teacher was a fine man and the students in that course were mostly high-school graduates so it was a good course. The other courses seem to be pretty good now, too—at least the school has a better reputation these days.

Taking the four cities together, trained youth tended to approximate the average for the whole youth group in scholastic abilities, as well as in social and economic backgrounds.

Education Completed

The youth were divided into three groups of roughly equal size— the eighth-grade graduating classes of 1929, 1931, and 1933. (See appendix table 6.) This basic prerequisite for inclusion in the sample, together with the fact that trained youth were defined as those who had completed at least one semester of secondary school study in a Smith-Hughes vocational program, explains the fact that few of the trained youth had received less than 9 years of schooling.

Vocationally trained youth were slightly below untrained youth in average amount of schooling completed in three of the four cities. This was only natural, since fewer of the trained youth took college preparatory work in high school and fewer went on to college.[6] On

---

[5] Of the trained youth, 18 percent received scores below 7 and only 6 percent rated 10 or more on the Stanford tests, which was over a year in advance of the "normal" attainment. Of the untrained youth, 28 percent received scores below 7, and 15 percent rated 10 or more.

[6] In St. Louis, for example, only 3 percent of the trained youth interviewed had completed 1 year or more of college, compared with 10 percent for untrained youth. It should be explained, however, that Smith-Hughes work was never tabulated in the present study as extending beyond the twelfth grade, so that youth who took postgraduate work in full-time Smith-Hughes programs would be shown as having completed only 12 years of school, unless they went on to college.

the other hand, only 3 percent of trained youth in St. Louis dropped out of school before completing the ninth grade, as compared with 28 percent of untrained youth in the same city. Thus the trained youth were predominantly an "average" group in amount of schooling, with few cases of extremely high or low educational attainment.[7] (See appendix table 7.)

Youth who completed their vocational training went further in school than those who failed to complete their programs. The former group averaged over 12 years of school completed, compared with only 11 years for those who dropped out of vocational school.

Composition of the Group

Most of the trained youth studied—57 percent—were young women. This compares with about 52 percent of young women among all youth interviewed in the same cities.[8] The actual proportions of young men and women varied greatly from city to city, however, according to the types of training offered. (See appendix table 8.) In Denver only boys had received training, because the only full-time Smith-Hughes programs offered at West High School were industrial in nature. In Birmingham 30 percent of the trained youth interviewed were girls, compared with 60 percent in St. Louis and 66 percent in Seattle. These differences in the sex composition of various trained groups must be kept in mind in all comparisons between trained and untrained youth, between trained youth in the different cities, and between youth in the various types of training programs. The sex factor is particularly important where earnings are under discussion.

Nearly all the youth studied (96 percent) were of the white race. In St. Louis about 13 percent of all white youth interviewed, compared with 10 percent of the Negro youth interviewed, had had Smith-Hughes work. No Smith-Hughes training was available to Negroes in the Birmingham secondary school system, in spite of the large size of the Negro group there. Negroes were therefore underrepresented in both St. Louis and Birmingham.

---

[7] In St. Louis well over half of the trained youth left school before completing the twelfth grade. An even greater proportion of untrained youth dropped out of school before finishing high school, however—58 percent as against 53 percent in St. Louis. As a result, trained youth in that city had, on the average, 7 or 8 months more education than untrained youth. In other words, although a larger proportion of untrained than of trained youth went to college, the average level of education in St. Louis was so low that in the process of attending vocational schools, the average trained youth passed the average level of educational attainment of untrained youth.

[8] See Payne, Stanley L., *Thirty Thousand Urban Youth*, Social Problem Series No. 6, Work Projects Administration, Federal Works Agency, Washington, D. C., 1940.

The average age of the vocationally trained youth varied from just under 21 to just over 22 years in the four cities at the time of interview (July 1, 1938). Ninety-seven percent of the trained group ranged from 18 to 24 years of age. (See appendix table 9.)

In summary, the characteristics of vocationally trained youth were not very different from those of other youth in the four cities covered by the present study. Such variations as did appear suggested that trained youth clustered more closely around the average than did other youth in terms of social backgrounds, scholastic aptitudes, and amounts of education. The principal differences between the two groups were that more of the trained than of the untrained youth were girls and were white youth.

WHERE THE YOUTH WERE TRAINED

There were wide variations among the four cities included in this survey in terms of the age, size, and scope of their respective vocational school systems. St. Louis had the oldest and largest system of vocational training of the four cities. Courses of a vocational nature were first introduced into the public schools of that city in 1907, and they came under the Smith-Hughes Act in 1922. In 1927 the present Hadley Vocational School was established for white students, and 2 years later the Booker T. Washington School was opened for Negroes, both under the Smith-Hughes plan. All full-time, day training programs have been given in these schools in recent years.

Denver had Smith-Hughes training as early as 1917, but only for evening and part-time work. From 1929 to July 1938, the period covered by the study, full-time Smith-Hughes industrial courses were given in West High School (where the Denver youth studied here were trained), but these courses have since been dropped. Seattle and Birmingham opened their present vocational schools in 1930.

A much higher percentage of all youth in St. Louis (all those interviewed in the survey of youth in the labor market) had had some full-time vocational work than had youth in the other cities.

Of every 100 youth interviewed in the original youth survey in:	The number having full-time vocational training was:
St. Louis	12
Birmingham	3
Denver	1
Seattle	3

The number of vocationally trained students actually interviewed in St. Louis was 2,461, compared with 293 in Seattle, 217 in Birmingham, and only 71 in Denver. St. Louis therefore bulks much larger in the present study than the other three cities combined.

THE NATURE OF THE TRAINING

There were considerable differences in the types of full-time programs offered under Smith-Hughes standards in the four cities. St. Louis offered the largest number of training programs, with Seattle and Birmingham next. Denver's West High School offered only three programs—auto mechanics, electricity, and machine shop—the only programs which were offered in all four of the survey cities.

Types of Programs

Over half of the trained youth had been registered in clerical or other white-collar programs. (The great majority of these were in St. Louis; the proportion of youth with such training was lower in the other three cities.) Most of the programs in this field were not financed with the help of· Federal funds; but all were taught under regulations similar to those which prevailed in the federally aided programs. About a third of the youth were in trade and industrial programs, and the remainder were in women's trades and the arts. (See appendix table 10.)

There was a sharp cleavage between the sexes in types of training. Girls made up the great majority of commercial students. Labor-market entrants with training in the industrial programs were males, with one exception; and those who had been in women's programs were females, with one exception. Students of both sexes were found in all of the principal commercial courses as well as in all of the arts programs. (See appendix table 11.)

Completion of Training

Only a little over a third of the trained youth [9] had actually completed their vocational studies. Failure to complete a program, however, did not necessarily denote lack of success in that field. Vocational training is training for jobs; and if youth were able to get jobs in their particular fields before finishing their programs, as was sometimes the case, they may perhaps be counted among the most successful.

Of the labor-market entrants, more girls than boys completed their training in the four cities combined—43 percent of the girls as against 32 percent of the boys (appendix table 11). The margin of difference in this direction was large in Seattle and St. Louis; but in Birmingham more boys than girls had completed their programs.

Among youth trained in:	Of every 100 boys, the number with completed training was:	Of every 100 girls, the number with completed training was:
St. Louis	28	40
Birmingham	52	38
Denver	29	—
Seattle	42	67

[9] See footnote 1, p. 11.

The youth who completed their training were, on the average, almost half a year younger at the time of their eighth-grade graduation and at the time of interview than the youth with incomplete training.[10] Negroes stayed with their training more frequently than whites; the smaller number of jobs available for Negro youth may have lessened the temptation for them to leave school.

There was a wide variation by program in the proportions of students following the training through to completion. Heading the list were students in cosmetology or beauty culture, 94 percent of whom completed their programs in St. Louis. Students in highly specialized courses, such as secretarial work and accounting in the commercial field, were more likely to complete their training than youth in less specialized programs. There were great variations among cities in the proportions of students completing comparable programs, probably because of conditions in the local labor markets—the demand for workers in certain fields, and the number of trained or partly trained workers available to fill that demand. Likewise there were great variations in proportions of youth completing different types of programs. In St. Louis 40 percent of the youth in commercial programs had completed their training, compared with only 24 percent of those in industrial programs. (See appendix table 12.)

The reason cited most often by youth for failure to complete their training programs was "preference for work."

Of every 100 youth who left vocational school before completing their programs, the following reason:	*Was given by this number:*
Preference for work	32
Lack of funds	28
Lack of interest	22
Preference for other types of education	6
Physical disability	2
Marriage	1
Other	9

The proportion of youth leaving vocational school before completing their programs because of "preference for work" was twice as large in St. Louis as in Denver. Financial reasons accounted for about a fourth of all withdrawals in every city.

The intermediate age group (1931 eighth-grade class), most of whom came into the labor market during the worst depression years (1932–1935), left school because of financial difficulties more frequently than did the youngest and oldest groups. Boys left school more often

---

[10] In Birmingham, where Stanford Achievement Test ratings were available, however, the youth who were 1 year below the norm in their scores proved most likely to complete their training. Over half of this group, compared with only a little more than a third of those who had scores above normal, finished their programs.

because of preference for work, and less often because of lack of interest, than girls. (See appendix table 13.)

Occupation of Father and Type of Training

The type of training acquired by youth was influenced to some extent by family occupational backgrounds. Youth whose fathers were professional or clerical workers were more likely to enroll in commercial training programs, and male youth from skilled, semi-skilled, and unskilled workers' families were more likely to go into trade and industrial programs, than the average. In St. Louis for example:

Of every 100 trained male youth whose fathers were:	*This number entered trade and industrial programs:*
Professional persons	41
Proprietors, managers, and officials	71
Clerical workers	58
Skilled workers	73
Semiskilled workers	78
Unskilled workers	77

Families in which the fathers were engaged in clerical occupations produced more than their share of accounting, secretarial, and drafting students—in fact, a greater number of such students than came from any other occupational group. Skilled workers' sons went in for woodwork and aeromechanics most frequently, supplying more students in these programs than did any other occupational group. The children of semiskilled workers were most likely to go into the machine-shop, electricity, aeromechanics, and clerical programs. Youth from unskilled workers' families tended to register for the sheet-metal, general commercial, cosmetology, and industrial sewing courses most frequently. (See appendix table 14.)

The importance of these differences may, however, be overemphasized. The most significant thing is that there was not a very strong tendency for youth to choose training similar to the occupations of their parents. The fact that almost half of the youth from semi-skilled and unskilled workers' families registered for commercial courses, for example, indicates that our system of free public vocational education leaves the door at least part way open for shifts in occupational status from generation to generation.

Chapter III

EMPLOYMENT AND EARNINGS OF TRAINED YOUTH

No OBJECTIVE evaluation of the results of vocational education is possible until the nature and purposes of such training are clearly defined. Vocational education, in its broadest meaning, includes all training and experience which help an individual to find a job and make a living. All education is vocational in this sense. But for practical purposes it is necessary to distinguish between general education and training aimed at fitting youth for specific types of work. Vocational training of the sort covered by the Smith-Hughes Act and other Federal legislation has been defined by the United States Office of Education simply as "training for useful employment."[1] If this definition is accepted, the results of training may best be stated in terms of the amount and types of useful employment obtained by vocationally trained youth.

The primary purpose of this chapter is to study the work histories of trained youth to determine the extent to which they have succeeded in getting and keeping jobs, and to compare trained youth with other youth with respect to their status in the labor market.

There are several difficulties to be overcome, or taken cognizance of, in any discussion of the results of vocational training. First, what criterion of "success" in the labor market is to be used? If employment is the criterion, should it be employment status at the time of the survey, or percent of labor-market time spent in employment during the entire period covered? Should principal stress be placed upon first jobs, jobs held at the time of interview, or all jobs? Should earnings be considered as approximately equal in importance to employment in measuring success in the labor market?

---

[1] Office of Education, *Statement of Policies for the Administration of Vocational Education*, Vocational Education Bulletin No. 1, General Series No. 1, Revised Edition, U. S. Department of the Interior, Washington, D. C., February 1937, p. 6.

Because of the inadequacy of any single one of these criteria, a multiple approach to the question is utilized in the following discussion. Both employment and earnings are examined from several different angles in order to obtain as complete and accurate an appraisal of the results of vocational training as possible.

A further question arises: Have the youth surveyed had time to make a satisfactory adjustment in the labor market? Most of them had been working or seeking work for several years at the time of the survey; but the unfavorable economic conditions which prevailed during the depression undoubtedly retarded them in getting jobs, especially jobs of the sort they desired. Many youth will make more satisfactory adjustments, particularly with regard to wages, as time goes on. This is true even in more prosperous times, however; and since untrained youth graduated from the eighth grade at the same time and were roughly of the same age as trained youth, comparisons between these two groups as to general employment status are valid.

It should be remembered that only one type of federally sponsored vocational training—full-time day-school training in Smith-Hughes programs—is under discussion in the present report. Several kinds of training are included in the program of the United States Office of Education.

Vocational education . . . may be given to boys and girls who, having selected a vocation, desire preparation for entering it as trained workers; to youths who, having already entered employment, seek greater efficiency in that employment; and to adult workers established in their trade or occupation who wish through increase in their efficiency and wage-earning capacity to advance to positions of responsibility. [2]

The first category of training referred to is that available in the regular day programs of the vocational high schools; the second and third types are represented by part-time, apprentice, and evening trade extension programs, which have a larger attendance than the day programs, especially in the industrial field. Data available from the present survey were limited to the first type of training mentioned.[3] The conclusions tentatively outlined below would therefore apply principally to this group.

It is possible that youth or older persons with part-time or extension training might have made a better showing than former day-school students in terms of employment, earnings, and relationship of jobs to training, because of their greater age and experience. Such persons were already in the labor market and at work before starting their

---

[2] *Ibid.*, p. 6.

[3] A minor exception is the inclusion of a few Seattle and Birmingham youth with training in distributive or business education programs which, although nominally on a part-time basis, are actually on a level fully comparable to full-time programs.

part-time training, and most of them had gone back to vocational school with the definite objective of improving their status on the job. Older part-time students in particular are a selected group, most of whom know rather specifically what they want to gain from additional schooling. Day-school students, in contrast, are often young, immature, and lacking in practical work experience to serve as a background for their vocational studies.

This section of the report, then, should be read with the realization that it does not presume to give complete or final answers to the whole question of the value of vocational training. Rather, it tells what happened during the depression to a representative group of youth with full-time training in four cities, and compares their work histories with those of youth without such training. Such differences as appear between trained and untrained youth do not necessarily mean that one type of education is superior to the other in preparing youth for the labor market. Too many factors are involved to permit such a generalization. Differences occur because a combination of several factors—notably the composition of the particular groups studied, the nature and quality of the education they received, and the state of the labor market—operates to the advantage of some youth and to the disadvantage of others in terms of employment and earnings.

The figures presented below, then, may be taken as indications of the results of full-time, day training programs operating under Smith-Hughes standards. Where trends are similar in all four cities, tentative generalizations may be made; but where the data are not in agreement, as is often the case, they are significant only as representing the city or cities where they were obtained.

LABOR-MARKET STATUS OF TRAINED YOUTH

In three of the four cities studied well over nine-tenths of all trained youth had entered the labor market at some time since leaving school.

Among trained youth in:	This number were interviewed:	This number had entered the labor market at some time:	Of every 100 this number had entered the labor market at some time:
All 4 cities	3, 042	2, 857	94
St. Louis	2, 461	2, 354	96
Birmingham	217	204	94
Denver	71	68	96
Seattle	293	231	79

There were two reasons for the relatively small proportion of labor-market entrants in Seattle: (1) Seattle youth went further in school than youth in any of the other three cities, and therefore had entered the labor market in fewer cases, on the average, than youth in the other cities. This was particularly true among youth with Smith-Hughes training because many students at Edison Vocational School had previously graduated from the regular high schools. (2) Seattle had a larger proportion of women among its trained youth than did the other cities; and in each city the proportion of women entering the labor market was somewhat lower than that of men.

In each of the cities except Seattle, youth with Smith-Hughes training not only entered the labor market, but also remained in the market in a much higher proportion of cases than was true of other youth. This was in spite of the fact that the trained group included a greater preponderance of young women.

Of every 100 youth:	This number had entered the labor market at some time:‧	This number was still in the labor market on July 1, 1938:
With Smith-Hughes training	94	81
Without Smith-Hughes training	85	67

There were sharp differences in the number of months spent in the labor market by trained youth in the four cities. In Denver they had spent almost twice as much time in the labor market as had youth in Seattle. There was no consistent difference between trained and untrained youth in total time spent in the labor market.

Among youth in:	The average (mean) number of months spent in the labor market by youth with	
	Smith-Hughes training was:	No Smith-Hughes training was:
St. Louis	42	49
Birmingham	37	33
Denver	47	36
Seattle	25	32

These differences in amount of labor-market experience, among cities and between trained and untrained youth, must be kept in mind in all comparisons of youth in the various cities or in the trained and untrained groups within the cities.

A smaller proportion of trained than of untrained youth were still in school at the time of interview, in three of the four cities.[4] Of Smith-Hughes youth 6 percent were in school, compared with 13 percent of the untrained youth, in the four cities combined.

Fewer Smith-Hughes youth than other youth were listed as "not seeking work," and therefore out of the labor market, in each city. Only one Smith-Hughes youth in eight was in this category, while the proportion was one in five among other youth. (See appendix table 15.)

---

[4] More of the trained than of the untrained group were in school, however, in Seattle.

Status in the Labor Market, 1929–1938

To get a clear picture as to when Smith-Hughes trained youth entered the labor market, it is necessary to examine the proportions of youth in school and in the labor market over a period of years. For this purpose the oldest group of trained youth, the eighth-grade class of 1929, was selected, since members of this class had been out of school longest and therefore the class presented the most comprehensive data on the transition from vocational school to employment or unemployment. (Figures 1A and 1B illustrate this process of transition. See also appendix table 16.)

The proportion of youth of this class in school gradually fell during the whole period covered, dropping from 100 percent in January 1929 to 5 percent or less from May 1936 on. The decrease was particularly great in 1933 (the normal year of high-school graduation for this group) and in 1934. Most of the youth first entered the labor market at the end of each school year, in June, while smaller groups left school each January.

It will be noted that there were surprisingly wide variations among these youth in time of leaving school. Some went into the labor market as early as 1929, although they had not had time to acquire more than one semester of vocational training at that time; many others stayed in school through 1934 or even later, although only 3 percent of all trained youth were recorded as having completed 1 year or more of college work. These apparent inconsistencies are explained by the fact that trained youth often entered the labor market for a time before or during their vocational school courses. This tendency to go back and forth between school and the labor market was much more prevalent among trained youth than among untrained youth.[5]

The principal difference between trained men and women of the 1929 eighth-grade class was the smaller proportion of young women in the labor market throughout the period studied. From 1934 on (when most of the girls had passed their eighteenth birthdays) the difference was accentuated by the increasing number of young women who left school or the labor market to become housewives.

The proportion of both sexes who were out of school but were neither working nor seeking work remained small but fairly constant throughout the period studied. This group included those who were physically unable to work, or those who, as in the case of many girls, were helping with the housework at home, or engaged in other unpaid family work.

[5] See Westefeld, Albert, *Getting Started: Urban Youth in the Labor Market*, Monograph No. XXVI, Division of Research, Work Projects Administration, Federal Works Agency, Washington, D. C., in preparation.

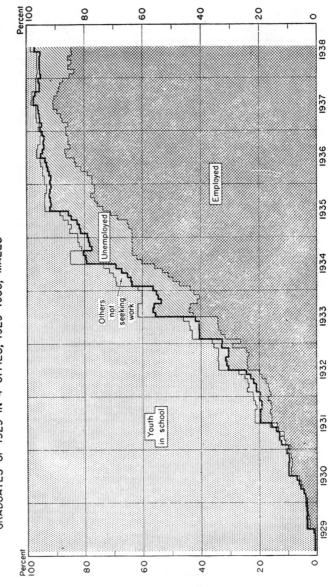

Fig. I A – LABOR-MARKET STATUS OF SMITH-HUGHES TRAINED YOUTH, EIGHTH-GRADE
GRADUATES OF 1929 IN 4 CITIES, 1929-1938, MALES

Source: Appendix table 16.

WPA 3757

Fig. 1B – LABOR-MARKET STATUS OF SMITH-HUGHES TRAINED YOUTH, EIGHTH-GRADE GRADUATES OF 1929 IN 4 CITIES, 1929-1938, FEMALES

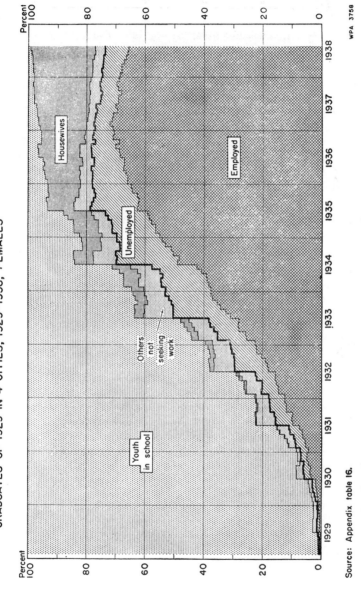

Source: Appendix table 16.

WPA 3758

The proportion of all trained youth who were employed increased fairly steadily during the period studied, at least until late in 1937. The proportion who were unemployed also increased, but only until 1935. In the period from 1935 to 1937 improved business conditions, combined with the increasing age and experience of the youth, produced a drop in unemployment among labor-market youth. From 1937 on, however, the downward trend in business activity caused a slight increase in unemployment. These trends are discussed in greater detail in the following chapter.

Trained youth of the eighth-grade classes of 1931 and 1933 followed the same general pattern as trained youth of the class of 1929, as far as entrance into the labor market was concerned. The incidence of employment and unemployment varied from class to class because of differences in age and labor-market experience, and because the impact of changing economic conditions came at slightly different points in relation to their entrance to the labor market. But the main outline of the transition from school to labor-market activities was so similar in the three classes that it is unnecessary to discuss the younger groups in detail.

Employment and Unemployment at Time of Interview

More than 8 out of 10 labor-market youth with some vocational training under the Smith-Hughes plan were working full or part time at the time of interview (on July 1, 1938).

Of every 100 trained youth in the labor market on July 1, 1938, in the 4 cities:
    82 were employed
        75 on full-time jobs,
        7 on part-time jobs;
    18 were unemployed

Denver had the largest proportion of young men employed, St. Louis the largest proportion of young women. Among trained youth in Birmingham and Seattle, young men had a definite advantage over young women in obtaining jobs; but in St. Louis there was little difference between the sexes in proportion of employment as of July 1, 1938. (See appendix table 17.)

Among trained youth in the labor market on July 1, 1938, in:	*Of every 100 males, the number employed was:*	*Of every 100 females, the number employed was:*
St. Louis	83	82
Birmingham	78	68
Denver (males only)	88	—
Seattle	81	75

The oldest youth, who had been in the labor market longest, had the most employment. The rising proportion of employment as youth grew older was a reflection of increasing maturity and experience. Youthful inexperience was apparently more of a handicap among trained girls than among trained boys.

Among trained labor-market youth who graduated from the eighth grade in:	Of every 100 males, the number employed on July 1, 1938, was:	Of every 100 females, the number employed on July 1, 1938, was:
1933 (youngest group) _____	75	59
1931 (intermediate group) _____	82	88
1929 (oldest group) _____	87	88

Trained Negro youth were unemployed and employed only part time in a much greater proportion of cases than trained white youth in St. Louis, the one city where it was possible to make a comparison between the races. Less than half as many Negroes as whites had full-time employment (30 hours or more per week). Four out of every ten Negro youth were totally unemployed, compared with one out of every six white youth. There can be little doubt that these differences in employment status resulted principally from the fact that Negroes are definitely handicapped as compared with whites in the search for jobs. (See appendix table 18.)

Completion of training was associated with a relatively high proportion of employment at the time of interview in Birmingham and Seattle,[6] though not in St. Louis.

Among trained youth in the labor market on July 1, 1938, in:	Of every 100 with completed training the number with jobs was:	Of every 100 with uncompleted training, the number with jobs was:
St. Louis_____	82	83
Birmingham_____	80	73
Denver_____	*	**85
Seattle_____	80	74

    *Less than 25 youth with completed training.
    **Less than 50 youth with uncompleted training.

The difference in job status between youth with completed and uncompleted training was even greater when only full-time jobs were taken into consideration. In Seattle, for example, 73 percent of the youth with completed training, but only 57 percent of those with uncompleted training, had full-time employment. (See appendix table 18.)

Nearly all of the trained labor-market youth who were unemployed were actively seeking private employment. Only a little more than a fiftieth of all trained youth, and an eighth of all those who were jobless, were on work programs—NYA, WPA, or CCC. In Denver, however, the number on projects was almost 6 percent of all trained youth (half of those without private employment). In St. Louis a

---

[6] A survey made by Seattle school authorities in February 1938 showed that 88 percent of the June 1937 graduates of day trade or industrial programs, and 72 percent of the graduates of the business training programs, were regularly employed. (Fleming, Samuel E., *The Story of the Thomas A. Edison Vocational School*, Washington State Planning Council, Olympia, Wash., Sept. 24, 1938, p. 14.)

sixth of all trained Negro youth—and almost half of those who were totally unemployed—were on work programs; but only 1.5 percent of all trained whites were so engaged.

It is interesting to note in this connection that the proportion of youth on work programs was almost twice as large among those with uncompleted training as among those who were fully trained. This was true in every city. Apparently many of the youth who left vocational school for financial or other reasons before completing their programs were from needy families eligible for work relief.

Earnings and Hours of Trained Youth

The earnings of trained youth were very low during the depression years covered by this study. One St. Louis youth who had studied commercial art and sign painting at Hadley Vocational School told the following story, which is quoted here to illustrate the effects of poor business conditions and extensive unemployment upon the wage levels of young workers:

Commercial art would be all right if you could land a job. The best way to do that is to get experience, and that means some sort of an apprenticeship. After I left Hadley I went to a fellow down on Delmar who's got a little art shop of his own and asked him for some kind of a job so I could learn more about the trade. Do you know what he said? He said he'd give me a job and pay me just carfare and lunch money. He said that was the best he could do because there was another fellow in the shop and business was so bad he was going to have to lay him off. I said nothing doing. I needed *money*.

After that I got a job writing signs for a big chain of grocery stores. I worked there 4 years, off and on, and always got $15 a week. I was in charge of sign-writing for 47 stores in St. Louis and over in Illinois, and I worked 60 hours a week, but a lot of times I had to put in 70 hours, with no extra pay for overtime. When I asked the boss, "Can't you do something about these long hours?" he said, "Sure we can do something; we can get someone to take your place if you can't stand the gaff."

Average weekly earnings for full-time jobs held at the time of interview by youth with Smith-Hughes training amounted to about $16.20 per week. Earnings were highest in Seattle for both males and females and lowest in St. Louis for males and in Birmingham for females.

Among trained youth with full-time jobs on July 1, 1938, in:	Average weekly earnings of males were:	Average weekly earnings of females were:
St. Louis	$18. 40	$15. 00
Birmingham	19. 00	13. 10
Denver (males only)	18. 90	—
Seattle	20. 20	15. 60

About one-twelfth of all trained youth with full-time jobs were earning $10 or less, more than four-tenths $15 or less, and only 11 percent $25 or more per week.

Trained Negro youth in St. Louis earned much less than trained white youth. Negroes earned an average of $10 per week on full-time jobs held at interview, compared with $16 for whites. The hourly earnings of the Negroes averaged 17 cents, compared with 37 cents for the whites.

Hours worked by all trained youth averaged about 43 per week on full-time jobs. The greatest range among the four cities was for young women, who worked an average of 42 hours per week on full-time jobs in Seattle and 50 hours per week in Birmingham. Negro youth worked much longer than white youth in St. Louis, averaging 60 hours per week as against 43 hours for the whites.

By far the largest number of trained youth—over half of all those employed 15 hours or more a week—were working from 40 to 44 hours per week. About 15 percent were working 50 hours or more per week. It is interesting to note that maximum earnings were found in the 40–44-hour group. Many youth who worked less than 40 hours were underemployed, while many of those working over 50 hours were in lines of work where hourly wages were very low.

Completion of vocational training appeared to give youth a definite advantage in terms of earning power in Birmingham, and a slight advantage in Denver; but in Seattle youth who left school before finishing their programs actually earned slightly more than other youth. Completion of training made no difference in earnings among St. Louis youth. (See appendix table 19.) The following figures are for all full-time jobs held at any time:

Among trained youth in:	Average weekly earnings among youth with completed training were:	Average weekly earnings among youth with uncompleted training were:
St. Louis	$14.70	$14.70
Birmingham	16.00	15.00
Denver	15.40	15.20
Seattle	15.00	15.30

The fact that more girls than boys completed their training in Seattle and St. Louis, while the opposite was true in Birmingham, is reflected in these figures. But in general it may be said that the advantage of longer experience in the labor market held by those who had left school before their programs were completed tended to offset the advantage of additional training on the part of those who had completed their programs, as far as earnings were concerned.

TRAINED YOUTH AND OTHER YOUTH COMPARED

In comparing youth with and without Smith-Hughes training, it should be remembered that the Smith-Hughes group included many youth—a majority of all those considered as "trained"—who did not complete their training programs. Likewise, the group without Smith-Hughes training—usually referred to for the sake of convenience as the "untrained" group—included some youth with vocational training in the private schools or with vocational courses in the regular high schools. It also included a few youth who had attended Smith-Hughes schools for less than one semester. The trained and untrained groups, then, were not as sharply differentiated from each other as these terms would indicate. Nevertheless, separation of youth with a semester or more of Smith-Hughes training from all other youth provides at least some basis for estimating the results of Smith-Hughes training as compared with other types of schooling.

Employment and Unemployment

Trained youth appeared to have a small advantage over untrained youth in terms of employment status as of July 1, 1938. In three of the four cities Smith-Hughes trained youth had a slightly higher proportion of employment and a lower proportion of unemployment than other youth. (In Seattle, where the opposite was true, trained youth had been in the labor market for an average of only 25 months, compared with 32 months for untrained youth.)

Among youth in the labor market on July 1, 1938, in:	Of every 100 with Smith-Hughes training the number who were employed was:	Of every 100 with no Smith-Hughes training the number who were employed was:
St. Louis	83	81
Birmingham	76	72
Denver (males only)	88	85
Seattle	78	82

The Sex Factor

These variations were partly the result of differences in the sex composition of the trained and untrained groups, especially in Denver and Birmingham, where males predominated, and in Seattle, where females predominated, in the trained groups. Taking the males only, those with training were on the whole slightly better off than those who were untrained. Seattle again was an exception, but the advantage of untrained youth there was narrower when young men were considered separately.

Among young men in the labor market on July 1, 1938, in:	Of every 100 with Smith-Hughes training the number employed was:	Of every 100 with no Smith-Hughes training the number employed was:
St. Louis	83	81
Birmingham	78	74
Denver	88	85
Seattle	81	83

A higher proportion of untrained women than of trained women were employed in two of the three cities where programs were available to women. In the third city, St. Louis, the opposite was true, but the difference was negligible. (See appendix table 17.)

Among young women in the labor market on July 1, 1938, in:	Of every 100 with Smith-Hughes training the number employed was:	Of every 100 with no Smith-Hughes training the number employed was:
St. Louis	82	81
Birmingham	68	70
Seattle	75	78

Full-Time Employment Only

When only full-time jobs (those averaging 30 hours or more per week) of youth of both sexes were considered, the difference in favor of trained youth in Birmingham increased, while the difference in favor of the Smith-Hughes group in Denver disappeared.

Among youth in the labor market on July 1, 1938, in:	Of every 100 with Smith-Hughes training the number with full-time jobs was:	Of every 100 with no Smith-Hughes training the number with full-time jobs was:
St. Louis	76	74
Birmingham	73	61
Denver	78	78
Seattle	67	70

The fact that all of the trained youth in Birmingham were white, while many of the youth without Smith-Hughes training were Negroes, was no doubt partly responsible for the wide difference in that city.[7]

Taking the four cities together, the chances of being employed at some sort of full-time job were about 4 percent better in the Smith-Hughes group than among the untrained youth.

Of every 100 labor-market youth in the 4 cities on July 1, 1938:	The number employed full-time was:	The number employed part-time was:
With Smith-Hughes training	75	7
Without Smith-Hughes training	71	9

[7] In Birmingham 39 percent of all Negro youth in the labor market, but only 23 percent of all whites (trained and untrained), were unemployed on July 1, 1938.

Youth With Smith-Hughes and Private School Training Compared

When the group without Smith-Hughes training was broken down into those with some vocational training in private schools and those with no training of a vocational nature whatsoever, the results were extremely interesting. About 3 percent more of Smith-Hughes trained youth were employed than of youth without any vocational training in public or private schools. But the Smith-Hughes group had somewhat less employment than youth with training in private vocational schools.

	The number employed on
Of every 100 labor-market youth with:	*July 1, 1938, was:*
Smith-Hughes training _____	82
Private vocational school training _____	87
No vocational training of any type in either public or private schools _____	79

This general picture was true in each of the four cities except Seattle, where the Smith-Hughes trained youth were at the bottom of the list in terms of employment.[8] (See appendix table 17.)

The most obvious conclusion would appear to be that as far as enabling youth to get jobs is concerned, Smith-Hughes training is better than no vocational training, but somewhat less effective than vocational training outside the public school system. Such a generalization is premature, however, until differences in amount of education in these groups are taken into account.

The Factor of Amount of Education

The average level of education of the Smith-Hughes group, as pointed out above, was definitely lower than that of other youth, with a much smaller percentage going on to college. But the untrained youth were a very heterogeneous group. Some of them had had professional training, which may have given them an advantage in qualifying for jobs. On the other hand, many had dropped out of school soon after graduating from the eighth grade, and their small amount of education may have put them at a disadvantage in getting jobs.

There are two major questions to be answered in connection with the educational factor: First, which was more effective in helping youth to get jobs, a period of vocational training or an equal period of experience in the labor market? Second, which type of schooling was the most productive of employment, a period of vocational training or an equal period spent in ordinary high school?

In order to provide tentative answers to these questions, St. Louis youth were studied, both because their large numbers enabled detailed comparisons to be made and because nearly all of their training was on a

---

[8] In Seattle, as mentioned above, Smith-Hughes trained youth had spent less time in the labor market than untrained youth, and were preponderantly girls.

high-school rather than a postgraduate level. First, Smith-Hughes youth were compared with untrained youth who had dropped out of school upon graduating from the eighth grade. The trained youth were divided into those with 10 or 11 years of education, many of whom had not completed their training; and those with 12 years of education, nearly all of whom had completed their vocational programs. A comparison of these two groups with the untrained youth who had dropped out of school without completing more than eight grades indicated that there was little difference in employment status between the trained and untrained youth, even though the latter had only a grade-school education.

Of every 100 St. Louis labor-market youth who were:	This many were employed on July 1, 1938:
Smith-Hughes youth who had completed 12 years of school only	80
Smith-Hughes youth who had completed 10 or 11 years of school only	83
Untrained youth who had completed 8 years of school only	82

Apparently labor-market experience was as valuable in terms of employment as vocational education, at least up to the time of interview. In fact, the additional year or two spent in the labor market by trained youth with only 10 or 11 years of school as compared with those with 12 years of school, appeared to give the trained group with the shorter period of schooling a slight advantage in getting work—an advantage which might easily have been overcome, however, as trained high-school graduates subsequently acquired more work experience. The small advantage held by the group with 10 or 11 years of education may also have arisen from the fact that some youth left school before they finished their programs because jobs were offered them at that time.

To provide an answer to the second question, youth who had completed 10 or 11 years of school and those who had finished high school were again singled out, this time from both the trained and the untrained groups. A comparison of these youth indicated that at the lower educational level, Smith-Hughes trained youth had the most employment.

Of every 100 St. Louis labor-market youth who had completed 10 or 11 years of school only, and who had:	The number who were employed on July 1, 1938, was:
Smith-Hughes training	83
No Smith-Hughes training	79

At the level of high-school graduation, however, untrained youth had a slight advantage over trained youth with the same amount of education.[9]

---

[9] Youth who went on to college were eliminated from both the trained and untrained groups of high-school graduates considered here so that the two groups were fully comparable in educational level.

Of every 100 St. Louis labor-market youth who had completed 12 years of school only, and who had:	*The number who were employed on July 1, 1938, was:*
Smith-Hughes training _____	80
No Smith-Hughes training _____	83

One reason for the slightly greater proportion of untrained high-school graduates than of Smith-Hughes trained graduates holding jobs may have been that most employers of white-collar workers preferred high-school graduates. Youth who failed to graduate from high school, and who also failed to acquire any vocational training, were probably at a disadvantage as compared with Smith-Hughes trained youth. Graduates of the nonvocational high schools, on the other hand, were apparently able to get jobs, particularly office and sales jobs, more readily than either untrained nongraduates or vocational school graduates. Many of the jobs held by untrained graduates, however, were in part-time, low-paid employment.[10]

Duration of Initial Unemployment

Smith-Hughes training made little difference in the amount of unemployment experienced by youth before they obtained their first jobs. In both the trained and untrained groups, one youth in five was unemployed for 6 weeks or less, and one in four for a year or more, before obtaining the first full-time job. Only in Seattle was there any considerable difference between the two groups. In that city only 12 percent of the trained youth, as against 19 percent of those without Smith-Hughes training, were unemployed for a year or more after leaving school before finding full-time jobs.

Duration of Jobs

Even after youth obtained their first jobs, the short duration of these jobs showed that there was a considerable "floundering period" between graduation from vocational school and fairly permanent placement. The average duration of first jobs of trained youth ranged from 3 months in Seattle to 6 months in St. Louis. About 1 first job in 10 in each city lasted less than a month. There was practically no difference between Smith-Hughes trained youth and other youth as far as the average duration of all jobs was concerned.

Proportion of Time Employed

When proportion of labor-market time spent in employment was considered, the Smith-Hughes group failed to show any considerable advantage over other youth except in Birmingham.

---

[10] There was a higher incidence of part-time employment among untrained than among trained youth. When part-time jobs were excluded, the trained and untrained high-school graduates were found to have had about the same proportion of employment.

Of each 100 months spent in the labor market by youth in:	The number of months spent in employment by Smith-Hughes trained youth was:	Other youth was:
St. Louis_____	79	80
Birmingham_____	84	76
Denver_____	87	86
Seattle_____	83	81

In Birmingham the presence of many Negroes in the untrained group probably accounted for most of the difference. In the other three cities trained youth had had about the same proportion of employment as other youth. (See appendix table 20.)

Earnings of Trained and Untrained Youth

The earnings of trained and untrained youth are not necessarily a good measure of the effectiveness of vocational training—at least not so good a measure as amount of employment. Many of the lines of work for which youth are trained in Smith-Hughes programs do not pay high wages; and yet if youth trained in these programs get jobs, particularly jobs in their fields of training, the main purpose of vocational training may be said to have been accomplished. In any comparison of trained and untrained youth, however, earnings must be taken into consideration if the picture is to be complete. The inclusion of earnings on full-time jobs held at the time of interview is particularly desirable, since they tell at least something of the ability of the youth to advance to more highly paid work after a considerable period in the labor market.

In Birmingham and Denver youth with Smith-Hughes training were earning an average of $2 to $3 per week more than other youth on all full-time jobs (those of 30 hours or more per week) at which they were working at the time of the survey. In Seattle, however, the reverse was true—Smith-Hughes youth were earning less than other youth; and in St. Louis there was practically no difference between the two categories. (See appendix table 21.)

Average weekly earnings on full-time jobs on July 1, 1938, in:	For Smith-Hughes trained youth were:	For other youth were:
St. Louis_____	$16. 00	$16. 10
Birmingham_____	18. 20	15. 20
Denver_____	18. 90	16. 80
Seattle_____	17. 90	19. 60

These figures do not take into account such important factors as the racial and sex composition of the trained and untrained groups. The high earnings of Smith-Hughes trained youth as compared with untrained youth in Birmingham are due largely to the fact that the

Smith-Hughes group there included only white youth, while a large proportion of the other youth were Negroes. When Negroes were eliminated from the untrained group, the average earnings of the remaining whites rose to $17.10, or to within about a dollar of the average earned by the white Smith-Hughes youth.[11] When the fact that most trained youth in Birmingham were young men is taken into account, the advantage held by trained youth decreases still further.

In Denver the higher earnings of Smith-Hughes trained youth were due to the fact that all were young men, with a differential advantage in earning power to begin with. When girls were eliminated from the untrained group, average earnings for the remaining males rose to about the same amount as the average for trained youth.

Sex and Earnings

A breakdown of earnings by sex shows not only the fact that there was a sharp differential in average wages between the sexes but also that training tended to benefit girls more than boys in terms of earnings. Trained males earned less than untrained males (except in Birmingham, where the trained group were all white youth), whereas trained females earned more than untrained females in St. Louis and Birmingham (though not in Seattle).

On full-time jobs on July 1, 1938, average weekly earnings of Young men in:	With Smith-Hughes training were:	With no Smith-Hughes training were:
St. Louis	$18. 40	$18. 60
Birmingham	19. 00	18. 00
Denver	18. 90	19. 00
Seattle	20. 20	23. 40
Young women in:		
St. Louis	15. 00	14. 40
Birmingham	13. 10	12. 30
Seattle	15. 60	16. 40

In St. Louis the young men with no training had a 20-cent advantage in average weekly earnings over those with training, while among the young women, those with training earned an average of 60 cents per week more than those without training. In Seattle untrained males had an apparent advantage of more than $3 in weekly earnings over trained males; but untrained females had an advantage of only 80

[11] Average weekly earnings of all white youth, trained and untrained, on full-time jobs held at the time of interview ($17.20) were twice as large as those of all Negro youth ($8.50) in Birmingham. About one-tenth of all white youth were earning $10 or less per week, compared with more than two-thirds of all Negroes. Similarly, a tenth of all vocationally trained youth were earning $10 or less per week, compared with a quarter of all youth without Smith-Hughes training.

cents per week over trained females.[12]   In Birmingham slightly higher earnings were apparent among trained youth of both sexes.[13]

Education and Earnings

Taking the combined factors of sex and amount of education into account, it appeared that as far as earnings were concerned, in St. Louis girls with Smith-Hughes training had a slight advantage over untrained girls who had left school upon completing the eighth grade. Young female workers with Smith-Hughes training who had completed 12 years of education earned an average of $15.40 per week, and those with 10 or 11 years of education earned an average of $14.60.   Young women with no Smith-Hughes training, and with only an eighth-grade education, earned an average of only $13.80.

Among the young men, however, the reverse was true.   Smith-Hughes trainees with 12 years of education earned an average of $18.10 per week, and those with 10 or 11 years of education $18.40, whereas untrained youth who had left school before completing the ninth grade earned an average of $19.60.   Apparently among the young men 2 to 4 years of vocational education was of less value in terms of earning power than an equal amount of time spent in the labor market.

It should be noted that youth who did not go on to high school were, on the average, older at the time of eighth-grade graduation than other youth.   Since among all male youth, trained and untrained, 4 years' additional age brought an average wage increase of more than $6 per week,[14] age was an important factor in determining earnings—apparently more important than training.   Among young women, however, there was a much smaller average increment in weekly earnings with age.   Therefore the greater average age of the girls with the lowest educational attainment did not offset the financial disadvantages associated with retardation in school, small total amount of education, and lack of specific training.

When groups of trained and untrained youth of both sexes with equal education were compared, this wage differential still persisted.   Among male youth who had completed 10 or 11 years of education, those with Smith-Hughes training earned an average of $18.40 per week on all full-time jobs held at the time of interview, while those without training

[12] As noted previously, the advantage held by untrained youth in Seattle may have been attributable partly to the longer period of time they had spent in the labor market.

[13] This advantage might be expected to disappear, however, if the factor of race were taken into account.

[14] Cf. Payne, Stanley L., *Thirty Thousand Urban Youth*, Social Problems Series Number 6, Work Projects Administration, Federal Works Agency Washington, D. C., 1940, p. 9.

earned $18.50. Among girls of the same educational level, those with training averaged $14.60. and those with no training $14.20.

At the twelfth-grade level, however, the Smith-Hughes group (nearly all of whom had completed their training) had a slight advantage over untrained youth of both sexes. The figures were $18.10 as against $17.60 for the young men, and $15.40 as against $15 for the young women.

Changes in Wage Levels

It might be argued that another survey of the same youth, made a few years later than the present one, would show that Smith-Hughes training gives men as well as women a definite advantage in earning power. Industrial training may not have its full effect, for example, until the youth with such training acquire some experience in their special fields. The present survey indicated, however, that any advantage ultimately shown as a result of training would probably be small. In fact, a study of job shifts (changes either in employment or in wage levels) showed that trained youth advanced to higher wage levels at about the same rate as other youth.

Of every 100 changes in jobs or wage levels among youth with:	The number resulting in higher pay was:	The number resulting in lower pay was:
Smith-Hughes training	61	25
No Smith-Highes training	60	28

Trained youth had a slight advantage over untrained youth in obtaining promotions to jobs paying higher wages in St. Louis and Seattle. In Birmingham, however, only 51 percent of the trained group improved their status when they made shifts in jobs, compared with 62 percent of other youth; and in Denver there was little difference between the two groups.

Hours of Work

There was practically no difference in working hours between trained and untrained youth, or between those who did and those who did not complete their training programs. In each of these groups the average was about 43 hours per week.

Summary

Considering all the evidence with regard to both employment and earnings, it can only be concluded that in the four cities studied there were no sharp differences in economic status between youth with Smith-Hughes vocational training and other youth.

Chapter IV

EMPLOYMENT IN RELATION TO
SPECIFIC TYPES OF TRAINING

IF VOCATIONAL training is defined as "training for useful employment," then the purpose of specific training programs or groups of
training programs is to prepare students for successful employment
in the particular fields of work for which they have been trained.
The value of a given training program to vocational students may
therefore be appraised primarily in terms of their success in obtaining
employment that bears some relationship to their training. Other
criteria to be considered relate to the ability of the youth to hold
their jobs and to earn adequate wages.

In the present survey data were gathered on types of employment
and weekly earnings of youth trained in the various Smith-Hughes
programs. An examination of these data indicates that there were
wide variations among students trained in the different programs, in
terms of employment in relation to training as well as in terms of
earnings and duration of jobs. Some programs were instrumental
in enabling a large proportion of youth to enter the fields of work
for which they had prepared themselves; others were less successful
in this respect.

In discussing the results of specific training programs in terms of
related employment it is especially important that the factor of time
in the labor market be kept in mind. A survey of these same young
people in 1941 might show a somewhat higher proportion of them in
employment related to their training than in 1938, for several reasons:
their increasing age and maturity, their more complete orientation
in the economic world, and the more favorable conditions existing
in the labor market subsequent to the 1938 survey. But the job
status of trained youth in any given program in relation to that of
trained youth in other programs would probably be about the same
in 1941 as in 1938.

More detailed information was available in St. Louis than in the other three cities, because of the comprehensive nature of the St. Louis vocational school system and the large number of youth trained therein. Fortunately, St. Louis has a widely diversified economic base, and therefore offers many types of employment to young people. Since quality of training and labor-market conditions varied from city to city, however, data for St. Louis programs were compared with data for similar programs in Birmingham, Denver, and Seattle whenever possible.[1]

EMPLOYMENT IN FIELD OF TRAINING

In order to estimate the extent to which youth obtained jobs in the specific fields for which they were trained, a detailed study was made of the types of jobs youth had held and of the relationship of such jobs to their training in each of the four cities.

Occupations of Youth in Relation to Training

Youth with some Smith-Hughes training were in general less likely to become unskilled workers on their first jobs, and more likely to be skilled, semiskilled, or clerical workers than were other youth. This is to be expected, since the function of vocational education is to prepare youth for jobs in these fields. Following is the occupationa' distribution of the trained youth on their first full-time jobs:

Of every 100 trained youth who obtained employment in the 4 cities:
     2 were professional workers,
     1 was a proprietor, manager, or official,
    48 were clerical workers,
     5 were skilled workers,
    33 were semiskilled workers, and
    11 were unskilled workers on their first jobs.

In each of the four cities a comparison of the first jobs and jobs held at the time of interview by trained youth showed that the number of youth in unskilled work decreased sharply with additional labor-market experience.[2] The number of youth in skilled work showed an increase from first jobs to jobs held at the time of interview, as did the number in semiskilled work in each city except St. Louis. (See appendix table 22.) At the time of interview there were more skilled and fewer unskilled workers among trained youth than among other youth in the four cities.

The large proportion of trained youth who went from school directly into clerical jobs is particularly significant. In spite of the

[1] Programs with fewer than 25 labor-market entrants in a given city were excluded from the detailed analysis.

[2] There was some overlapping between first jobs and jobs held at the time of interview (on July 1, 1938).

common notion that there is a great oversupply of clerical workers, a large majority of the employed youth with commercial training were successful in getting clerical or other "white-collar" work. In St. Louis of every 100 youth with commercial training who got jobs, 72 became "clerical or kindred workers" on their first jobs. (See appendix table 23.) The proportion of commercial trainees who were in clerical work increased to 76 percent on jobs held at time of interview.[3] (See appendix table 24.) It should be mentioned, however, that not all clerical jobs were related to the specific types of commercial training the youth had acquired.

Among St. Louis youth with training in industrial programs only 12 out of 100 first jobs were in skilled work, and 48 were in semiskilled work. The number in skilled work increased to 17 in 100, and the number in semiskilled and unskilled work decreased slightly on jobs held at interview.

Method Used in Relating Specific Jobs to Training

To arrive at a fair estimate of the effect of vocational training in enabling youth to get jobs in the specific lines of work for which they were trained, it was necessary to make a more precise comparison of training programs and individual jobs than was possible on the basis of the broad occupational groupings cited above. The comparison of each of the various jobs at which youth had worked since leaving school with the training of these same youth required the tabulation of all the various combinations of training and jobs. With both occupation and industry taken into consideration, each job was then classified as having (1) a primary or direct relationsip, (2) a secondary relationship, or (3) no relationship at all to the youth's training. For example, in the case of girls trained as stenographers, such jobs as stenographer, secretary, and dictaphone operator were classified as directly related to the training program involved. Other clerical jobs, such as bookkeeper, comptometer operator, multigraph operator, mail clerk, and file clerk, were classified as having only an indirect or secondary relationship to stenographic training. Occupations such as beauty operator, waitress, and housemaid were classified as having no relationship to stenographic training.

In the industrial programs it was more difficult to determine the precise relationship of jobs to training. Often the industry where the youth worked, as well as his occupation, was taken into consideration. In the case of a youth with training in auto mechanics such jobs as apprentice mechanic, auto mechanic's helper, grease man, and filling station proprietor were considered to bear a primary or close relationship

---

[3] In Seattle, where a highly specialized business training course was given, 70 percent of all first jobs and over 90 percent of all jobs held at time of interview by youth who had taken this course were in clerical occupations.

to the training the youth had received. Such jobs as chauffeur, electrician, and machinist's helper, which involved work related to some degree to a course or courses within the auto mechanics training program, were considered to bear a secondary relationship to the same field of training. Likewise, the proprietor of a used-car lot, although not engaged in auto-repair work, was classed as working at a job indirectly related to his training as a mechanic. If a youth worked as grocery salesman, office clerk, messenger, bookkeeper, or in any other nonmechanical type of work, however, his job was considered to be unrelated to the auto mechancis training program.

After tentative decisions had been made as to each job's relationship to the training of the youth who held that job, the entire list of decisions was checked by experts on the subject of vocational training in the United States Office of Education. Their modifications of the original decisions were then incorporated into the procedure for classifying the jobs.

Vocational Training in Relation to Types of Employment

Each youth's work history was classified according to the types of employment he had had. It was found that almost three-fifths of all trained youth who had been in the labor market had had one job or more with at least some relationship to their training. In the other two-fifths of the cases the youth had had no employment in their fields of training or no jobs of 15 hours or more per week.

Of every 100 youth with Smith-Hughes vocational training who had entered the labor market,

46 had had jobs closely related to their fields of training;
13 had had jobs with only a secondary relationship to their training;
33 had had only jobs with no relationship to their training; and
8 had had no jobs of 15 hours or more per week by July 1, 1938.

These figures give only a general picture of what happened to trained youth after they left school. The proportion of youth who obtained related jobs varied from city to city, of course. (See appendix table 25.)

Of every 100 trained youth in the labor market in:	*This number had had jobs with some relationship to their training:*	*This number had had only jobs with no relationship to their training:*
St. Louis	59	33
Birmingham	58	37
Denver	40	54
Seattle	62	20

In every city except Seattle the proportion of trained labor-market youth who had never had a job of 15 hours or more per week was less than 8 percent. In the Pacific coast city, however, 18 percent had had no jobs. This was probably because Seattle youth, as mentioned above, had been in the labor market for a much shorter period than had youth in the other three cities.

Young women with training had a slight advantage over trained young men in getting jobs in their fields of training, in two of the three cities where training was offered to both sexes.

Among trained labor-market youth in:	Of every 100 young men, the number who had had employment related to their training was:	Of every 100 young women, the number who had had employment related to their training was:
St. Louis	56	62
Birmingham	58	58
Seattle	60	63

Completion of training had a great effect on the type of work obtained in each of the four cities. Three-fourths of all labor-market entrants who finished their training programs got jobs with at least some relationship to their training; but only half of those who had dropped out of their training programs had ever held related jobs. This was in spite of the fact that those who had dropped out were in the labor market an average of 10 months longer than those who stayed with their training to completion.

Among labor-market youth in:	Of every 100 with completed training, the number who had related jobs was:	Of every 100 with uncompleted training, the number who had had related jobs was:
St. Louis	74	51
Birmingham	68	49
Denver	60	31
Seattle	78	40

Trained youth as a group had spent an average (mean) of 40 months in the labor market, of which 14 months, or a little more than a third of their labor-market time, was spent in employment related to their training. Those who had completed their training programs, however, had related jobs during more than half of the period when they were in the labor market.

Of every 100 months spent in the labor market by:	The number of months spent in employment related to their training was:
All trained youth in the 4 cities	36
Youth with completed training	54
Youth with uncompleted training	28

This greater success of youth with completed training in getting appropriate employment may have been partly a reflection of the fact that vocational schools assumed some responsibility for placing their graduates in jobs, while nongraduates had to shift for themselves in the labor market. It may also be a result of the fact that youth who were least interested, or who showed the least ability, in the training programs they entered, were the ones who tended to drop out; these youth could hardly have been expected to get jobs related to their training as frequently as fully trained youth, since their occupational preferences and abilities were apt to lie in other fields. But certainly the greater adequacy of completed training had something to do with the greater ability of youth with such training to get jobs in their respective fields.

Young men appeared to benefit in terms of related employment as a result of completion of training more consistently than did young women in the three cities where training was given to both sexes on a full-time basis. This may have been partly because most boys went into industrial programs, and most girls into commercial programs. Completion of training was more closely associated with success in obtaining related employment in the case of industrial programs than in the case of commercial programs.

Among youth in:	Of every 100 young men, the number who had had related jobs was:	Of every 100 young women, the number who had had related jobs was:
St Louis		
With completed training	76	74
With uncompleted training	48	54
Birmingham		
With completed training	71	57
With uncompleted training	44	59
Seattle		
With completed training	69	81
With uncompleted training	53	27

In Seattle and St. Louis young women apparently were greatly aided in obtaining related employment by completion of training, but in Birmingham no such tendency was apparent.

Individual Training Programs in Relation to Types of Employment

There were wide differences, in terms of success in finding employment related to their training, among youth who had graduated from the various training programs. The following quotation from a St. Louis girl with commercial training illustrates this variation:

The school got me my first job, and I've always had work as a typist or stenographer. . . . Most of the people I know who went to Hadley have jobs now, but, of course, some of them don't have the kind of jobs they want. I know three boys who graduated from Hadley at the same time I did. One of them took drafting, and he's pressing pants in a cleaning shop. Another took auto mechanics, and he's labeling boxes in a big cigar store. The other one took printing and he's a printer now. He only makes $16 a week, but I guess that's all right; he's learning the trade, and he'll probably go on up.

At the top of the list in terms of employment bearing some relationship to training were youth (all girls) trained in cosmetology or beauty culture. More than eight-tenths of these girls, in both St. Louis and Seattle, had found jobs in beauty parlors. At the other end of the scale were St. Louis woodworkers, show-card writers, and sheet-metal workers, of whom not more than a third had found work with any apparent relationship to their fields of training.

Differences of this sort depend on several things. First, the number of jobs and the number of trained youth available to take them—that is, the state of the labor market—determine to a great extent the success a youth will have in finding the type of job he wants. (Sheet-metal work was scarce because of the drop in building and other construction during the depression, while work in beauty shops was relatively little affected.) Second, the degree of efficiency attained by the vocational schools, and by teachers in those schools—the quality of instruction and equipment and the closeness of their relationship to local industry and the local labor market—may determine whether youth will be able to qualify for jobs in their fields.

A third factor also enters into any analysis of the relationship between training and employment. By definition, "related" jobs are jobs in which youth can use to some extent the training they received in their respective vocational programs. But some programs are related to a larger number of occupations than others. For example, a youth trained in show-card writing has a limited field of employment in which he can use his training, even if jobs bearing only a secondary relationship to this training—window-display work, for example—are taken into account. But a youth trained in auto mechanics may use some portion of his training not only in auto-assembly plants, garages, filling stations, and auto-wrecking establishments, but also in any one of a large array of jobs bearing at least a slight relationship to his training—including airplane construction, electric repair work, Diesel engineering, machine-shop work, and truck driving. The proportion of youth who had obtained jobs which were related to their training therefore depended not only on the quality of the vocational training received and on the state of the labor market during the period studied, but also on the scope of the related employment field.

TRAINING AND EMPLOYMENT IN ST. LOUIS

Since St. Louis, with 2,354 labor-market entrants among the trained youth interviewed, bulked much larger than the other three cities combined, most of the analysis of individual training programs in relation to type of employment is of necessity based on data gathered there. For the sake of convenience in treating the data, the St. Louis programs were divided into four main types: commercial programs, industrial programs, those which for want of a better name are termed "women's programs," and arts programs. (See appendix table 26.) In order to make the relative effectiveness of the different types of training stand out, the individual training programs were analyzed with regard to employment directly related to training. The following tables, unless otherwise specified, are based on the work histories of all trained youth in the various fields, whether or not their training was completed.

Commercial Programs

In St. Louis the 1,348 labor-market youth who had been trained in commercial programs had the best records in securing employment related to their training. Most of these youth (85 percent) were girls. Of each 100 commercially trained youth who had entered the labor market, 63 had held related employment, 50 in jobs closely connected with their training. Of the remaining youth, 28 had had only unrelated employment, and 9 no jobs of 15 hours or more per week. Among commercial students, the more highly specialized programs seemed to be most productive of employment in the immediate field of training.

Of every 100 St. Louis labor-market youth trained in:	The number who had held jobs directly related to their training was:
Special commercial	64
Secretarial work	58
Accounting	*51
General business	50
Stenography	42
General commercial	38
Clerical	35

*More than 25 but less than 50 youth.

Special commercial training, which heads the list, consisted of several short, intensive courses of a year or less each, stressing miscellaneous business-machine operations and general office procedure, but including also accounting and secretarial work in some cases. Because of the scope of the training and the large number of related jobs, not only in general clerking and bookkeeping but also in stenography and the operation of office machinery, it was much easier for students with special commercial training to get related jobs than it was for those who had been limited to clerical training, which included typing, bookkeeping, and office practice but not office-machine work.

Although the comparatively specialized stenographic program showed up as less effective than the general business program in

" . . . *youth who had been trained in commercial programs had the best records in securing employment related to their training.*"

fitting youth for directly related jobs, this is not true if all related jobs are taken into account. The reason for this is obvious. Almost every office or clerical job may be said to be closely related to the general business program; in fact, only 3 percent of all youth with this training had had jobs that could be considered to have a secondary but not a primary relationship to their vocational studies. Among youth trained in stenography, however, jobs had to include typing and shorthand or dictaphone work to be classed as directly related to this training, and only 42 percent had had such employment; but another 24 percent had held jobs with a secondary relationship to their training—as office clerks, bookkeepers, or office-machine operators, for example. Including all related employment, then, two-thirds of the youth with stenographic training who entered the labor market had such work, compared with a little over half of those trained in the general business program.

Completion of training was an important factor in enabling commercially trained youth to get related jobs. (See appendix table 27.) Of the 40 percent who had finished their programs, more than three-fifths had at some time held directly related jobs; but of those who failed to complete their training, only slightly more than/ two-fifths had had such jobs. The differential was particularly great among youth trained in stenography; 59 percent of those with completed training, but only 32 percent of the others, had had employment in which they were able to use their training to any marked degree.

Industrial Programs

The 699 St. Louis labor-market youth with training in the trade or industrial programs, all but 1 of whom were young men, did not fare so well as the youth with commercial training in obtaining related jobs.

Of every 100 labor-market entrants among youth trained in industrial programs, 54 had had employment in which they used their training, 40 of these in work that was directly related to their programs. Young men with training in the machine-shop program were most likely to have done work that was directly related to their training, even in cases where the training program was not completed. Printing and electricity came next. At the bottom of the list were former students of woodworking and sheet-metal work, who for the most part found employment only in unrelated fields. (Fewer youth completed their training in sheet-metal work and woodworking than in any of the other programs; the proportion was 5 percent or less in these two programs.)

Of every 100 St. Louis labor-market youth trained in:	*The number who had held directly related jobs was:*
Machine shop	63
Printing	*58
Electricity	48
Drafting	36
Aero mechanics	*28
Auto mechanics	28
Woodworking	19
Sheet-metal work	14

* More than 25 but less than 50 youth.

Aeromechanics and auto mechanics fared somewhat better than these figures would indicate, for youth in both of these groups found considerable additional work that was indirectly related to their training. For example, the auto mechanics had worked as chauffeurs, machinists, air-conditioning and sheet-metal workers, coil winders, and toolmakers and diemakers; the aeromechanics had worked as motor and carburetor inspectors in auto-assembly plants, molders' and machinists' apprentices in metal shops, and in one case, as a business-machine serviceman; and both aeromechanics and auto mechanics had done bicycle and electrical repair work and had operated drill presses. All of these jobs had at least an indirect relationship to the training programs under discussion. Including all such employment, 61 percent of the youth trained as aeromechanics and 54 percent of those trained as auto mechanics had had work related to their training.

Again, youth who had completed their training had much better records than other youth. Only 24 percent of the youth with industrial training had finished their programs; and of these, almost two-thirds of all labor-market entrants had held directly related jobs by the time of interview, compared with less than one-third of those with uncompleted training.

Women's Programs

Youth who had been trained in cosmetology, industrial sewing, and similar programs had held jobs related to their training in about the same proportion of cases as had youth with industrial training. All but 1 of the 216 labor-market youth trained in such programs were girls.

Of every 100 young labor-market entrants with any training in these programs, 54 had had related employment, 51 of these in jobs closely associated with their training. If cosmetology, which had an extremely high rate of related employment, is excluded, however, the records of these girls show less employment that was associated to some degree with their training.

Of every 100 St. Louis labor-market youth trained in:	*The number who had held directly related jobs was:*
Cosmetology	*83
Industrial sewing	46
Cafeteria-tearoom	*30

*More than 25 but less than 50 youth.

It should be remarked that except for 15 percent of the youth with cafeteria-tearoom training, none of the young women trained in these programs had held jobs with only a secondary relationship to their training. In the cosmetology and industrial sewing programs the line was sharply drawn between directly related and unrelated employment, and there were no borderline jobs.

About two-fifths of the youth with training in women's programs had completed their training; and of these, 66 percent had had directly related jobs, compared with 41 percent of those who had not completed their programs.

Arts Programs

Youth with training in the arts programs, who numbered 91 labor-market entrants, had on the whole less related employment than any major St. Louis group with Smith-Hughes training. Some 63 percent of these youth were young men; almost nine-tenths of those who had taken show-card writing, and close to half of the commercial arts students, were males.

Taking all the former art students together, whether or not they had completed their programs, 52 percent had held related employment, 38 percent in jobs directly related to their training. Exactly half of the 54 former commercial arts students had had jobs that were directly related to their training; but only 6 of the 33 who had studied show-card writing (18 percent) had found jobs in that line of work. In the latter case, a few additional youth found jobs in window-display work, but even including these, only a third had held related jobs.

A third of the youth trained in the arts programs (about half of the commercial artists, but only a tenth of the show-card writers) had completed their training; of these, 55 percent had obtained directly related jobs, compared with 28 percent of those with uncompleted programs.

Race Differences in Obtaining Related Jobs

Negro youth in St. Louis obtained employment related to their training much less frequently than did white youth. Only a third of the 104 trained Negroes interviewed had obtained employment of the sort for which they had been specifically trained, compared with almost half of the 2,250 trained white youth. Among the trained Negro youth, 4 out of every 10 had never had jobs of 15 hours or more per week, while only 1 white youth in 16 had been entirely without such jobs. (See appendix table 28.)

Only 2 programs or groups of programs offered at Booker T. Washington School for Negroes had more than 25 registrants among the youth studied here, so that a detailed study of all programs was impossible. Such figures as were available indicated that Negro youth were at a severe disadvantage in the labor market compared with white youth as far as obtaining white-collar jobs was concerned.

Among youth trained in:	Of every 100 white youth, the number who had held directly related employment was:	Of every 100 Negro youth the number who had held directly related employment was:
Commercial programs	51	*20
Women's programs	51	52

* More than 25 but less than 50 youth.

In the general commercial program 112 out of 225 white youth, but only 9 out of 39 Negro youth, had had related jobs. In the women's programs as a group, however, there was little difference between the races in ability to get appropriate jobs. In cosmetology 21 out of 23 white girls got jobs in beauty shops, compared with 18 out of 24 Negro girls.

The effects of the depression were felt more sharply by Negro youth than by white youth. According to one St. Louis Negro boy:

Times are too hard to get a regular job. Lots of colored boys who finish high school go to Booker T. Washington vocational school afterward because they can't get jobs and there's nothing else to do. I got the notion to take printing at Booker T. because my cousin works in a little printing shop around here. He makes pretty good money, and I hung around the shop and got the idea I wanted to be a printer, too. So I took a 4-year course at Booker T. There wasn't much equipment in those days, but the teachers were fine. I learned to block out copy, set type, and operate the flat presses and the hand presses; and I took English, general science, math and history. I got my diploma in 1937.

But I couldn't get a steady job in printing or in any other kind of work. The teachers try to place the boys, but there are never many requests for printers. They did get me a part-time job at Goodwill Industries. For awhile I worked there 1 or 2 days a week, setting up and printing letterheads and cards, but that gave out. I put in applications at the State employment office and the Urban League, the only places where colored folks can go for jobs. But nothing happened, so about a year ago I went up to the NYA people and they put me on. I make $25 a month, working on a project at the "Y," and I've saved up $40.

I thought for a while I might go to Chicago; I've heard there are 20 printing shops there that employ colored workers, and there are only about 5 here in St. Louis. But that would take a lot of money, and times are hard everywhere. I'd rather save up enough money to set up a little print shop here some day.

RESULTS OF TRAINING IN CITIES OTHER THAN ST. LOUIS

In the other three cities there were only a few training programs with a sufficient number of youth to enable any detailed analysis to be made of work histories in relation to training. The results of these programs in terms of employment in related fields may well be examined, however, to see how the figures compare with those for St. Louis.

Seattle

The 231 labor-market youth with Smith-Hughes training in Seattle fared about as well as St. Louis youth. Of every 100 Seattle trained youth who entered the labor market, 62 had found employment in which they could use their vocational education, 55 of these in jobs directly related to their training.

In Seattle, as in St. Louis, students of beauty culture (cosmetology) did comparatively well; 81 percent of them got directly related jobs. There was little difference between the two cities in the proportion of youth with business training who had held directly related jobs; the figure was 52 percent in Seattle against 50 percent in St. Louis.

As in St. Louis, Seattle youth with commercial training, almost nine-tenths of them girls, had slightly more employment that was directly related to their training than had industrially trained youth. But youth trained in the women's programs (including 11 young men trained in the tailoring and dry-cleaning programs, but principally girls trained in courses concerned with clothing, food, home service and beauty culture) had had directly related employment in a larger proportion of cases than youth in either of the other types of programs.

Of every 100 Seattle labor-market youth trained in:	The number who had held directly related jobs was:	The number who had held only indirectly related jobs was:
Commercial programs	51	3
Industrial programs	47	19
Women's programs	62	3

When indirectly related jobs were combined with those bearing a direct relationship to training, both industrial and women's programs stood out above commercial programs. But this was true only because almost a third of the commercially trained labor-market entrants had never had a job on which they worked 15 hours or more per week. When these youth were eliminated in each group, commercially trained youth had had related jobs in a greater proportion of cases than youth in either of the other two categories of training.

There were sharp differences between Seattle and St. Louis with regard to the work histories of youth trained in certain comparable programs. Of the 21 Seattle labor-market youth trained in auto mechanics, 15 had had employment related to their training, compared with only 62 out of 114 St. Louis labor-market youth with similar training. In power or industrial sewing, 18 out of 23 Seattle girls with this training who entered the labor market had obtained related employment, compared with only 48 out of 103 St. Louis girls thus trained. In the latter program the difference may be accounted for at least in part by the fact that three-fourths of the Seattle girls, but only a little over one-fourth of the St. Louis girls, had completed the program. In the case of the auto mechanics, however, the proportion of Seattle youth with completed training was not much higher than that of St. Louis youth.

These divergencies between Seattle and St. Louis youth in two parallel programs may be due to differences between the labor markets in the two localities as well as to differences in number of youth completing the programs. It is probable, however, that the highly selective policy pursued in Edison Vocational School also reacted to the benefit of the Seattle youth. The number of vocational students trained there, as noted above, is rigidly limited to conform to estimated labor-market needs, and only the best equipped youth are admitted to the vocational programs. Seattle had less than a fourth as many youth as St. Louis in each of these two programs.

Birmingham

On the average, the 204 trained labor-market entrants studied in Birmingham fell slightly below those in St. Louis in terms of success in getting related jobs. Of every 100 who entered the labor market, 59 had found related employment, 42 of these in jobs directly related to their training (appendix table 26).

In Birmingham young men trained in the industrial programs had had directly related employment in a higher proportion of cases than youth trained in commercial or women's programs. When indirectly related programs were included, however, commercially trained youth (most of them trained in retailing) had had the most related employment.

Of every 100 Birmingham youth trained in:	The number who had held directly related jobs was:	The number who had held only indirectly related jobs was:
Commercial programs*_____	32	38
Industrial programs_____	44	13
Women's programs*_____	35	19

* More than 25 but less than 50 youth.

Of the 31 Birmingham labor-market youth trained in retailing, 11 had had directly related employment. Another 13 had had employment of a sort indirectly related to their training—chiefly in retail stores, at work other than salesmanship. More than three-fourths of all those trained in retailing had thus had employment with some relationship to their training.

Of the 24 Birmingham youth trained in machine shop, 19 had obtained related jobs. This was a larger proportion than in any other program in the city, and was slightly higher than the proportion of St. Louis youth trained in machine shop who had found related employment. Only 7 out of 20 Birmingham youth trained in printing, however, had held jobs in which they were able to use their training. This was a much lower proportion than that which was obtained among St. Louis youth with similar training. In other Birmingham programs too few youth had been trained to permit even a tentative evaluation of the results of training.

Denver

Vocational training in Denver's West High School was less productive of related employment than was the case in the other three cities. All of the 68 trained labor-market entrants studied there were young men, and only 20 had completed their training, which may help to explain the low relationship between training and jobs. Of the trained youth 27 got related employment, 17 in jobs directly related to their training.

All of the Denver youth had received industrial training. The 36 trained auto mechanics had slightly better success than the average trained youth in Denver in obtaining related jobs. The Denver youth studied were so few in number, however, that no definite conclusion can be drawn from their work histories.

Summary and Comparison of the Four Cities

When the four cities are compared many inconsistencies appear, but a few general trends are worth citing. Girls, on the average, had more success than young men in getting jobs associated with their training, and programs in which mainly girls were trained had the best records in this respect. Programs in which a large number of youth completed their training also ranked high.

Topping the list in terms of related jobs was cosmetology in both St. Louis and Seattle. Youth with commercial training fared surprisingly well in getting employment for which they were trained, in view of the large number with such training and the prevalent view that too many youth are preparing themselves for white-collar jobs. They compared favorably with youth who had had other types of training in all three cities where commercial programs were offered.[4] Youth with relatively specialized commercial training, such as that offered in the special commercial program in St. Louis, showed a high degree of ability to get related jobs; those with commercial training of a more general sort had the least success in this respect.

In the trade and industrial programs young men with training as machinists seemed to have an advantage over other industrially trained youth, particularly in St. Louis and Birmingham. Following are the figures on the three programs which were given in all four cities:

---

[4] In a recent study of Philadelphia public vocational school graduates similar conclusions were reached. Of the business graduates of 1935 who were employed 2 years later, 80 percent were in clerical or sales work in which they utilized the training they had received; of the employed graduates of the industrial curriculum, only 63 percent were in jobs related to their training. (Pavan, Ann, "A Follow-up Study of Philadelphia Public School Graduates, 1935," *Occupations*, Vol. XVI, No. 3, December 1937, p. 257.

Of every 100 youth in the four cities trained in the following programs:	This number had held directly related jobs:	This number had held only indirectly related jobs:
Machine shop	59	13
Electricity	46	10
Auto mechanics	32	24

Printing, which was offered in 3 of the 4 cities, was second only to the machinist program in terms of directly related employment, with 55 percent of all youth trained in this field having held directly related jobs. Young men with training of the type associated with building construction—woodworking in St. Louis and Birmingham, sheet-metal work in St. Louis—had the smallest proportion of directly related employment of all groups trained in industrial programs.

The percentage of youth completing specialized types of programs, particularly in the commercial field, was much higher than the percentage completing the more generalized programs. The greater chance of getting jobs in the more specialized types of work probably encouraged these same students to finish their training; and once they had graduated, they found that their completed training was especially helpful to them. Youth in the more general training programs, on the other hand, were more likely to become discouraged at the limited opportunities offered to them and to drop out of school. This put them at an added disadvantage.

TRENDS IN RELATED EMPLOYMENT, 1930–1938

Thus far the analysis of vocational training and its results in terms of actual jobs held has been based on the work histories of trained youth, in terms of whether at any time the youth had had employment related to their training. If the problems of vocationally trained youth during a depression period are to be understood, however, it is necessary to determine the employment status of such youth at various times over a period of years. In order to accomplish this, the activities of the trained youth on the first of each month were tabulated for the four cities together.

The Class of 1929

To standardize as far as possible the variable factors of age and experience, youth who had graduated from the eighth grade in 1929 were first studied separately from the others. A majority of them had left school between 1932 and 1934, when depression conditions were at their worst. They had subsequently spent an average of 5 years in the labor market. The collective experiences of these youth, who were on the average a little more than 23 years of age in 1938, form a significant index of employment among vocationally trained youth during the depression years. (See figures 2A, 2B, and 2C and appendix table 29.)

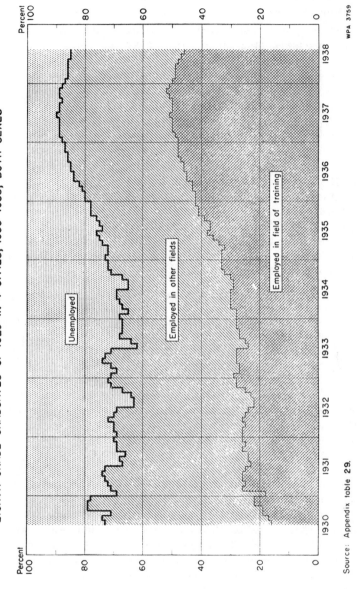

Fig. 2 A – EMPLOYMENT STATUS OF SMITH-HUGHES TRAINED LABOR-MARKET YOUTH, EIGHTH-GRADE GRADUATES OF 1929 IN 4 CITIES, 1930-1938, BOTH SEXES

Unemployed

Employed in other fields

Employed in field of training

Source: Appendix table 29.

WPA 3759

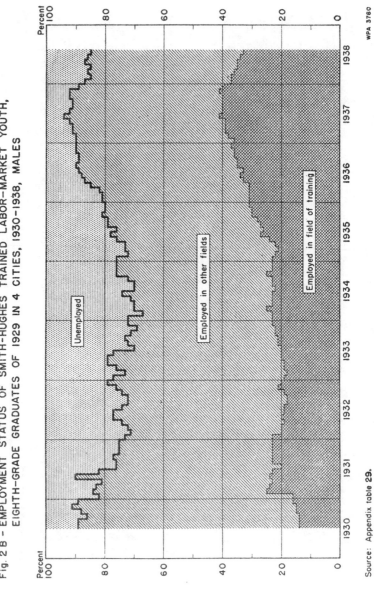

Fig. 2 B – EMPLOYMENT STATUS OF SMITH-HUGHES TRAINED LABOR-MARKET YOUTH, EIGHTH-GRADE GRADUATES OF 1929 IN 4 CITIES, 1930-1938, MALES

Source: Appendix table 29.

WPA 3780

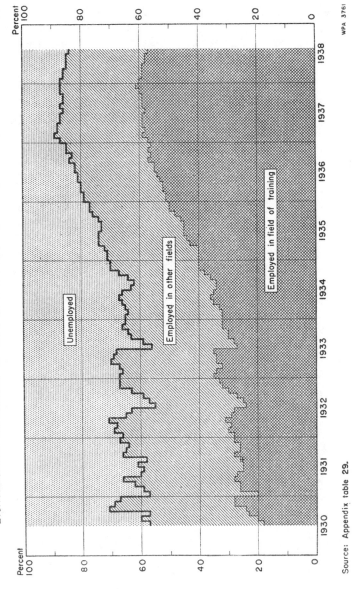

Fig. 2 C – EMPLOYMENT STATUS OF SMITH-HUGHES TRAINED LABOR-MARKET YOUTH, EIGHTH-GRADE GRADUATES OF 1929 IN 4 CITIES, 1930-1938, FEMALES

Unemployed

Employed in other fields

Employed in field of training

Source: Appendix table 29.

WPA 3761

The first fact which stands out from these data is that the proportion of labor-market youth whose employment was related to their fields of training, both directly and indirectly, increased fairly steadily month by month from 1930 through 1937, rising from a fourth to a half of all such youth.[5] During the first few years the upward trend in related employment was rather irregular; the proportion dropped slightly each July, when a new group of youth left school to enter the labor market. But the general tendency toward more employment of a sort that was related, directly or indirectly, to training was definite and unmistakable. The proportion of youth with employment that was not related to their training, on the other hand, decreased slightly in the first 4 years of the period studied, but stayed fairly constant from 1934 on.

Unemployment among the trained youth ranged from 21 percent to almost 40 percent during the period July 1930–July 1933. It dropped steadily thereafter until the end of 1937, then increased slightly during the first half of 1938. Unemployment thus reflected the general state of business activity during the 8-year period, falling to a minimum of 10 percent of all trained labor-market youth in the relatively prosperous year 1937. Both total employment and employment related to field of training reached their peaks in that same year, and more of the employed youth were working in related fields in 1937 than at any other time.

Employment related to fields of training tended to increase at the expense of unemployment during the period covered by these data, while employment unrelated to training remained about the same. This fact suggests that employment in related fields was dependent upon general business conditions to a greater extent than were other types of employment. In good times youth were best able to obtain jobs of the sort which they desired and for which they were trained. This was particularly true when the trend of the business cycle was upward.

There was a sharp difference between young men and young women in terms of employment related to field of training. A much higher percentage of girls than of young men had related jobs throughout the period studied. The percent of young men with related jobs rose from 14 to 41, while the percent of young women in such jobs rose from 18 to about 61, from 1933 through 1937.

This difference is partly explained by variations in training and in job opportunities between the sexes. Not only is the range of jobs that are related to specific industrial training programs somewhat narrower than in the case of commercial and women's programs, but

---

[5] In a few cases youth obtained their first jobs before taking vocational courses, then returned to school for specialized training.

also the total number of occupations open to young men is much greater than the number open to young women. Thus young men had a greater chance of getting unrelated work. The apparent advantage held by young women in obtaining employment related to their training throughout the period studied was therefore to some extent the result of differences in types of training and in occupational opportunities opened to young men and young women.

The Class of 1933

As a check upon the employment trends shown by the work histories of the older youth (1929 eighth-grade graduates), similar time-series data were compiled for the youngest group (the 1933 eighth-grade graduates). The two groups showed marked similarity in that both had an increasing amount of employment related to field of training as they spent more and more time in the labor market; but there were also sharp differences between them. (See figures 3A, 3B, and 3C and appendix table 30.)

In the first place, fewer of the 1933 than of the 1929 eighth-grade graduates left school at an early age to enter the labor market. This was particularly true among the girls; only about half as many of the 1933 class as of the 1929 class had entered the labor market a year after the date of their eighth-grade graduations.

Fig. 3 A – EMPLOYMENT STATUS OF SMITH-HUGHES TRAINED LABOR-MARKET YOUTH, EIGHTH-GRADE GRADUATES OF 1933 IN 4 CITIES, 1934-1938, BOTH SEXES

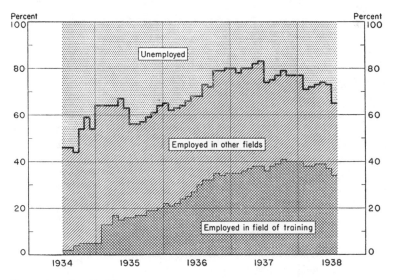

Source: Appendix table 30.

WPA 3762

Fig. 3 B – EMPLOYMENT STATUS OF SMITH-HUGHES TRAINED LABOR-
MARKET YOUTH, EIGHTH-GRADE GRADUATES OF 1933 IN
4 CITIES, 1934-1938, MALES

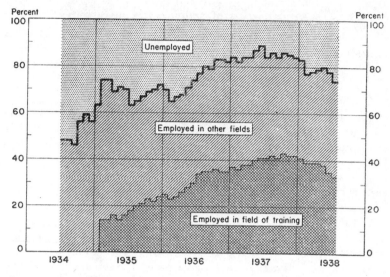

Source: Appendix table 30.

WPA 3763

Fig. 3 C – EMPLOYMENT STATUS OF SMITH-HUGHES TRAINED LABOR-
MARKET YOUTH, EIGHTH-GRADE GRADUATES OF 1933 IN
4 CITIES, 1935-1938, FEMALES

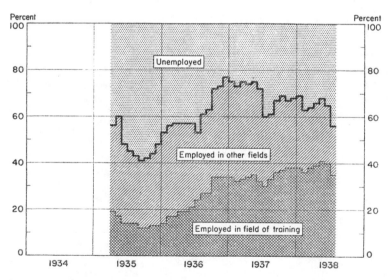

Source: Appendix table 30.

WPA 3764

A second difference was that fewer of the 1933 class members than of the 1929 class members who left school after only a year or two of secondary school training obtained employment related to their training. Evidently completion of training was more important as a prerequisite to securing related employment in the years 1934 and 1935 than in 1930 and 1931. Again, this was particularly true of the girls; 2 years after their respective eighth-grade graduating dates, 25 percent of the girls in the 1929 class who entered the labor market, but only 14 percent of those in the 1933 class, had related jobs. In the 1933 class, unlike the 1929 class, the girls had less related employment than the boys during most of the period studied.

The younger group (the 1933 class) showed a sharper and more consistent rise in proportion of related employment than did the older group during their first few years in the labor market. The 1933 class had 2 percent of its labor-market entrants in related employment in July 1934 and 30 percent in July 1936, while the 1929 class had 16 percent in related employment in July 1930, but only 22 percent in July 1932. The reason for this was that the younger group entered the labor market at a more favorable period of the business cycle—a time when general economic conditions combined with the increasing training, experience, and maturity of the youth to give them a better chance to secure jobs of the sort for which they were trained.

Finally, unemployment was more prevalent in the younger group than in the older one at the depth of the depression, because of the comparative lack of maturity and experience on the part of the 1933 graduates at that time. The recession of 1937–1938 hit the younger group hardest for the same reasons. Some of them were entering the labor market for the first time as late as 1937 and 1938, and new labor-market entrants are particularly handicapped when jobs are scarce. But there was no greater proportion of unemployment among 1933 class members in 1938 than there had been among 1929 class members in 1934.

Reasons for Increase in Related Employment

The generally upward trend in employment related to training in both classes and both sexes was due to three main factors: First, the training itself undoubtedly gave youth some advantage in securing the particular types of work for which they had studied. As time went on, youth tended to leave jobs which they looked upon as temporary stopgaps in order to get jobs in their fields of training. In other words, the effects of training were cumulative, and were not fully apparent until youth had had a chance to shift from makeshift jobs into jobs more to their liking. Furthermore, youth who came into the labor market several years after their eighth-grade graduation were better trained, on the average, than youth who started working or seeking work at an earlier date. Few members of the 1929 eighth-grade class who entered the labor market as early as 1930 or 1931 had completed their training, since most of the vocational programs in each of the cities required at least 2 or 3 years of general and specialized work for completion. From 1933 on, however, most of the new entrants into the labor market from this older group had finished their programs. As the percent of youth with completed training increased in the labor-market group, the proportion with related jobs also increased; this indicates that youth with completed training were better prepared to enter related employment than were other youth.

Second, increasing maturity and experience also helped youth to get jobs, especially jobs of their own choosing. Whether this factor was as important as training is difficult to say; but certainly age and experience were great assets to youth.

Finally, as noted above, improved business conditions had an obvious beneficial effect on employment opportunities of youth, whether or not they had received vocational training. In addition, in relatively prosperous times youth were best able to get the specific types of jobs for which they had been trained.

It is impossible to determine the extent to which each of these factors was responsible for increasing employment in fields of training. Probably all were important. Their combined effect, at any rate, was to enable more and more trained labor-market youth to get jobs appropriate to their training as time went on.

JOBS IN RELATION TO TRAINING

In order to determine more precisely the relationship between training on the one hand and employment status, duration of jobs, and earnings on the other, some of the data gathered in the present survey were tabulated on a job basis. By this means it was possible to determine the proportion of jobs directly and indirectly related, or unrelated, to the training of the youth who had held them. It was also possible to compare first jobs with jobs held on July 1, 1938, to determine trends, particularly with respect to earnings and duration of jobs.

First Jobs and Jobs Held at Interview

Since the time-series data in the previous section demonstrated that a steadily increasing proportion of all trained youth tended to get employment related to their vocational school work, a comparison of first jobs and jobs held at time of interview [6] would be expected to

---

[6] Youth with one job only are included in both groups—first jobs and jobs held at time of interview—in this section of the report. The latter are defined as all full-time jobs held on July 1, 1938. The number of jobs held at interview was smaller than the number of first jobs because a number of youth had left the labor market by July 1938.

show that a larger proportion of the latter than of the former jobs would be in fields related to the training of the youth. This was true, although the difference was not very great. (See appendix table 31.) It should be noted in this connection that the job data were for all three graduating classes combined. Thus the first jobs included not only those held in the years 1930 and 1931 (by 1929 eighth-grade graduates whose training programs were incomplete), but also many jobs held as recently as 1937 by youth with completed training.

Youth with completed training showed a greater increase in proportion of related jobs from first job to job held at interview than did those whose training was not completed. The proportion of directly related first jobs was twice as high among youth who had completed their training as among those with uncompleted training in each city. The same was true of jobs held at interview, in each city except Birmingham.

Among youth in the 4 cities whose training was:	Of every 100 first jobs, the number directly related was:	Of every 100 jobs held at interview, the number directly related was:
Complete	53	58
Incomplete	27	29

In Seattle, where the differences were greatest, well over half of all first jobs of youth with completed training were in directly related fields, compared with only a fifth of those held by youth who did not finish their programs. Seven-tenths of all jobs held at interview by Seattle youth with completed training, and less than two-fifths of those held by youth who failed to complete their programs, were in directly related fields.

The most precise method of analyzing jobs in relation to training programs is to determine the proportion of the youth with completed training programs who went into work directly related to their training. Only a few programs, however, had 25 youth or more with completed training who were recorded as holding jobs at the time of interview. (See appendix table 32.) Following are the figures for the more important programs in St. Louis:

Among St. Louis youth with completed training in:	Of every 100 first jobs, the number directly related was:	Of every 100 jobs held at interview, the number directly related was:
Commercial programs:		
Special commercial	71	78
Secretarial	48	58
Stenography	45	50
Industrial programs:		
Machine shop	*75	*65
Electricity	*62	*63
Women's programs:		
Cosmetology	*87	*84
*More than 25 but less than 50 jobs.		

When only youth with completed training were considered, special commercial training seemed to be more productive of directly related employment than any other program except cosmetology, as would be expected from the data previously presented Among the industrial programs the machine-shop program again led, with three-fourths of all first jobs of youth with this sort of training in machine-shop work, tool- and die-making, operating drill or punch presses, assembling motors or brakes, or other directly related work.

St. Louis youth with commercial training showed a definite tendency toward more employment in their special fields as time went on. This was not true, however, of industrially trained youth. And in the two programs with the largest proportion of initial employment in field of training—cosmetology and machine shop—there was a drop in directly related employment from first jobs to jobs held at time of interview.

In nearly every St. Louis program completion of training proved to be closely associated with success in obtaining related jobs. There was one exception: Youth with secretarial training, regardless of whether or not their training was completed, obtained directly related employment in about half of all first jobs and almost three-fifths of all jobs held at time of interview. In other commercial programs, and in all industrial programs, however, completion of training was highly important as a prerequisite to obtaining employment of a nature closely related to that training.

DURATION OF JOBS

Average duration of first jobs held by trained youth ranged from 3 to 6 months, and that of jobs at which the youth were still working on July 1, 1938, ranged from 12 to 18 months in the various cities. Jobs in the fields for which the youth were trained lasted longer on the average than other jobs in each city except Birmingham, where there was no difference between these categories. Jobs of youth who had completed their training lasted slightly longer than those of youth who had left school before completing their programs in St. Louis and Seattle, but not in Birmingham. (See appendix table 33.) Youth with completed training had, on the average, jobs of longer duration than those of untrained youth; and youth with uncompleted training had jobs of shorter duration than those of untrained youth. Again, this was true in each city except Birmingham.

There were some variations in terms of average duration of jobs among the different types of training programs. Commercial students had shorter first jobs and longer jobs held at time of interview than any other group in St. Louis.

Among St. Louis youth trained in:	The average duration of first of 2 or more jobs in months was:	The average duration of last of 2 or more jobs in months was:
Commercial programs	5	19
Industrial programs	8	16
Women's programs	7	12
Arts programs	6	13

Young women with training in cafeteria-tearoom work and young men who had been trained as draftsmen had the longest first jobs. Youth with general commercial and stenographic training had a slight advantage, however, in average length of jobs held at interview.

A larger proportion of time was spent in employment by youth trained in industrial programs than by youth trained in commercial programs, as a glance at the more important programs of each type will indicate.

Among St. Louis labor-market entrants with training in:	The average (mean) percent of total labor-market time spent in employment was:
Commercial programs:	
Secretarial	82
Stenography	81
Special commercial	76
General business	76
General commercial	75
Industrial programs:	
Printing	86
Machine shop	83
Auto mechanics	82
Electricity	82
Woodworking	79

Youth who had been trained in the secretarial and stenographic programs were better able to hold jobs than were general commercial trainees. This was in spite of the fact that youth with secretarial training had been in the labor market for only a little over 2 years, on the average, while those with general commercial training had been working or seeking work for over 4 years—almost twice as long. Among industrially trained youth students of printing and machine shop had the best success in holding jobs. (See appendix table 34.)

EARNINGS

Wages of youth trained in the various programs showed wide variations. This was to be expected, since wage levels in the various types of work for which they were trained varied greatly. A girl who completed a course in cafeteria-tearoom work and who obtained work in this field, for example, would hardly expect to earn as high wages as a boy who graduated from the machine-shop program and got a job as a skilled or semiskilled worker in industry. Both sex and occupational wage differentials are involved here. Earnings alone are not, therefore, a fair gauge of the relative effectiveness of various types of training.

Nevertheless average weekly wages are worth considering as one measure of success in the labor market. In this connection, although wage differentials on all jobs are given below, stress is placed upon differences between earnings on first jobs and jobs held at time of interview, and on differences between earnings on jobs related to training and other jobs, rather than on absolute figures. The results of such comparisons have at least some bearing on the relationship of different types of vocational training to earning power.

Weekly Earnings on All Full-Time Jobs

In St. Louis industrially trained youth had the highest earnings, with youth trained in the arts programs taking second place, when all full-time jobs were tabulated together.

Among St. Louis youth trained in:	Average weekly earnings on all full-time jobs were:
Industrial programs	$16. 20
Arts programs	15. 10
Commercial programs	14. 20
Women's programs	12. 40

These variations were largely the result of sex differentials in earnings. As noted previously, with one exception, only boys entered the industrial programs, which had the highest average earnings; and except for one boy, only girls were in the "women's programs," which had the lowest earnings. The other groups of programs were intermediate with respect to both sex composition and earnings.

Among industrially trained youth those trained as draftsmen earned the highest average weekly wages ($17.40), with former students of electricity and auto mechanics coming next. Lowest earnings in this group of programs were those of youth trained in printing, who earned an average of $14.90 on all jobs. (See appendix table 35.)

Among arts students, show-card writers, with average weekly earnings of $15.40, topped commercial artists, who averaged $14.60 on all jobs.

Youth who had studied accounting did best among commercially trained workers, with earnings averaging $16.40 per week. Bringing up the rear in this category were the youth with relatively unspecialized training—those from the general commercial and clerical programs, who averaged only a little over $13 per week.

" . . . *industrially trained youth had the highest earnings* . . . "

The youth with the lowest earnings of all groups, significantly enough, were young women trained in cosmetology. Although these youth had the best record of all groups in securing jobs in their field of training, their wages averaged less than $11 per week. (Similarly low wages prevailed among girls trained in beauty culture in Seattle; beauty operators in that city reported earnings varying from $6 to $15 per week.) St. Louis cosmetologists also had by far the longest working hours of all trained groups studied. Their hours averaged 55 per week, compared with only 44 for the next highest group.

In Birmingham highest average earnings were found among youth trained as machinists. In Seattle youth trained as machinists and as auto mechanics had the highest wages. But these averages were subject to a considerable degree of error because they were based on jobs held by fewer than 25 youth in each case.

Earnings on First Jobs and Jobs Held at Time of Interview

When first jobs and jobs held at time of interview of youth with two full-time jobs or more were considered, it was found that there was a sharp rise in earnings from first jobs to jobs held at time of interview, as would be expected. Part of this increase, however, was due to the fact that the proportion of girls was higher on first jobs than on jobs held at time of interview; many young women who had held two jobs or more had left the labor market by 1938.

Among trained youth in:	Average weekly earnings on first of 2 jobs or more were:	Average weekly earnings on last of 2 jobs or more were:
St. Louis	$12. 80	$16. 30
Birmingham	12. 40	18. 30
Denver	13. 70	19. 20
Seattle	13. 80	18. 60

These increases in average earnings did not, so far as could be determined, differ markedly from those of untrained youth. Exactly comparable figures are not available for youth with no Smith-Hughes training; but among all youth in the seven cities where the larger survey of youth in the labor market was conducted, average earnings rose from $14.20 on all first jobs to $17.70 on all jobs held at the time of interview. This increase of $3.50 in average earnings was the same as the increase which occurred from first to last of two jobs or more held by trained youth in St. Louis, although less than the increase in the other three cities. If the overlapping of first and final jobs among all youth had been removed, however, as was done in the case of the trained youth by eliminating youth who had held one job only, the increase in average earnings for all youth would probably have approximated the increases reported by trained youth in the four cities.

In St. Louis the sharpest increases from first to last jobs were among youth with training in the arts programs.

Among St. Louis youth trained in:	Average weekly earnings on first of 2 jobs or more were:	Average weekly earnings on last of 2 jobs or more were:
Arts programs	$13. 60	$19. 90
Industrial programs	14. 10	19. 10
Commercial programs	12. 60	15. 40
Women's programs	11. 00	14. 00

Here again, youth trained in women's and commercial programs were at a disadvantage. Not only did they receive a lower starting wage, but also they had less to look forward to in the way of increased earnings as time went on, than did other trained youth. The fact that most of those who had been trained in these programs were girls, except for a small proportion of young men in the commercial programs, undoubtedly had much to do with this.

It is significant that youth trained in the commercial programs had obtained related employment in a larger number of cases than had youth with other types of training, yet showed the smallest increase in earnings from first to last job. Furthermore, the largest wage increases were among youth trained in woodworking, show-card writing, and sheet-metal work, in the order named; and these were the very programs with the smallest number of youth who had ever had jobs in their fields of training. The smallest increase in average earnings, on the other hand, was among young women trained in cosmetology—the group who had had by far the greatest success in finding places in their fields of training. They started work at an average wage of $10 per week, and were earning only about $11.50 by the end of the survey period.

Earnings on Related and Unrelated Jobs

Wages of youth were not consistently higher in the lines of work for which they had been trained than in other fields. Earnings on all full-time jobs that were directly related to the training of the youth holding them were slightly higher than earnings on other jobs in both Birmingham and St. Louis; but this was not true in the other two cities.

Among trained youth in:	Average weekly earnings on all jobs: Directly related to training were:	With no relationship to training were:
St. Louis	$14. 90	$14. 20
Birmingham	16. 10	15. 30
Denver	13. 50	15. 30
Seattle	15. 00	15. 10

There was no consistent relationship, then, between high wages and employment in field of training.

There were differences among the various types of programs in this respect, however. St. Louis youth trained in the commercial and industrial programs derived a considerable financial advantage from employment directly related to their training as compared with employment in other fields, while girls trained in the various women's programs earned no more on jobs for which they had been trained than on other jobs.

Among St. Louis youth with training in:	Average weekly earnings on all jobs:	
	Directly related to training were:	With no relationship to training were:
Industrial programs	$16. 90	$15. 40
Commercial programs	14. 80	13. 30
Arts programs	15. 10	14. 70
Women's programs	12. 40	12. 40

Former students of auto mechanics, electricity, and machine shop showed the largest earnings of all groups on jobs within their fields of training, and also larger earnings in directly related than in unrelated types of work. Former students of cafeteria-tearoom work, printing, and accounting, on the other hand, earned more when they were working on jobs outside their training fields than they did when they were on jobs directly related to their training. In certain fields the best earnings were from jobs with a secondary relationship to training, rather than from those either with a primary relationship or with no relationship at all. This was true of the stenographic, secretarial, and accounting programs in the commercial field; and of the drafting, electrical, and auto mechanics programs in the industrial field.

Earnings and Completion of Training

There was no consistent relationship between completion of training and average weekly earnings, from program to program. For example:

Average weekly earnings of St. Louis youth trained in:	With completed training were:	With uncompleted training were:
Industrial programs	$16. 00	$16. 20
Arts programs	15. 00	15. 10
Commercial programs	14. 50	14. 10
Women's programs	11. 30	13. 00

Completion of training was most valuable to youth in the auto mechanics and stenographic programs in St. Louis. Girls with completed training in the women's programs, on the other hand, earned less than did girls who failed to complete these same programs, particularly in the cafeteria-tearoom and industrial sewing programs. One explanation for this is that the latter are relatively low-paid types of work, and those who left school to take jobs in other fields were therefore likely to earn more than if they had completed their programs and found work in their fields of training.

Summary

According to the present survey, Smith-Hughes trained youth earned no more than other youth; their earnings increased during the period covered by the survey, but probably no faster than those of other youth; they earned little if any more on jobs directly related to their training than they did on other jobs; and completion of training programs made little difference in their earnings.

Birmingham was the only city where the internal evidence on earnings suggested that vocational training might be productive of higher wages. In that city youth with completed training earned more than those who had attended only part of a program; all trained youth increased their average earnings almost 50 percent from first to last jobs; and they also earned a considerably higher weekly wage in jobs with a primary relationship to their training than in jobs with only a secondary relationship or no relationship at all. But it will be remembered that when trained and untrained youth were compared in Birmingham, the difference in earnings was small after the factors of sex and race had been taken into account.

In the other three cities vocational training did not have any consistent relationship to earning power. This was hardly surprising. For one thing, vocational training on the secondary school level does not pretend to train youth for high-paid jobs, but only for moderately skilled and semiskilled work; the group with Smith-Hughes training would therefore be likely to be limited to young people with medium or low earnings. It must also be kept in mind that the state of the labor market tended to depress the average earnings of trained youth, as well as those of untrained youth, during the depression.

CONCLUSIONS

There was little agreement among the various criteria of effectiveness of vocational training, with one or two exceptions. In the commercial field in St. Louis training in the more specialized programs, such as secretarial and special commercial work, resulted in the largest proportion of labor-market time employed, the largest proportion of youth with employment in related fields, and the highest wages. In the industrial field in St. Louis there was a slight positive relationship between employment in lines of work for which youth had been trained and percent of labor-market time employed; but there was no consistent relationship between related employment and duration of jobs or earnings. (See appendix table 36.) In Denver trained youth had less related employment than in any other city; yet they had more total employment than in any other city, and their earnings were relatively high.

In summarizing the last two chapters, it may be stated that vocationally trained youth as a group did not differ appreciably from other youth in amount of employment or in earning power. A detailed examination of programs indicated that in a few fields of work prospects for employment and for relatively high wages were enhanced by training, especially if that training was completed. Such variations depended to a great extent on local labor-market conditions. Probably in more prosperous times more of the trained youth would have found related employment. But in a depression labor market, when jobs of all kinds were scarce, trained youth had about as much difficulty in becoming adjusted economically as did youth with education of a less specialized sort.

Chapter V

VOCATIONAL TRAINING OUTSIDE THE SMITH-HUGHES SYSTEM

THE FEDERALLY aided system of vocational education is the most highly developed and carefully standardized type of vocational training available in public schools throughout the country. There are, however, several other sorts of training of a vocational nature, both in the public schools and elsewhere. Many regular high schools offer orientation courses of a vocational or prevocational type. Parochial schools in some cities have similar courses. Apprentice systems sponsored by unions and employers offer practical vocational training and experience. Training of workers on the job, by a process of "upgrading" or by short-term training courses in private factories, has become increasingly important since the defense program has created shortages of certain types of skilled workers. Finally, in every city there are numerous private schools and colleges which offer specialized vocational courses. These latter range from business colleges and trade institutes to schools and academies that offer professional training, such as schools for artists, dentists, and nurses.

In the present survey some data were obtained on vocational training of two types other than Smith-Hughes training: vocational training in the regular high-school system (data obtained in Seattle only), and training in private vocational schools (data obtained in all four cities). Because of the limited amount of material available, the analysis of these types of vocational training is of necessity less detailed than the analysis of Smith-Hughes training. The general results of regular high-school and private school vocational training will be of interest, however, in connection with the analysis of the results of Smith-Hughes training presented above.

TRAINING IN THE REGULAR HIGH SCHOOLS OF SEATTLE

In each of the four cities studied there were some "prevocational" courses offered in the regular high schools, aside from Smith-Hughes programs in the vocational schools. In three of the cities this training was not sufficiently specialized or extensive to be comparable to the training offered under the provisions of the Smith-Hughes Act. Accordingly, vocational training was limited by definition to Smith-Hughes training in these cities.

In Seattle, however, vocational courses were well attended and well developed throughout the regular junior and senior high-school systems. This resulted in part from restrictions placed upon admittance to Edison Vocational School, the one school where Smith-Hughes training was offered; these restrictions led many students, who would otherwise have gone to Edison, to stay in the regular high schools and register for vocational courses there. Graduates of vocational-type courses in the regular high schools of Seattle were classed by school officials as "vocationally trained" if they had received a specified number of semesters of training in a given field. Thus, youth with only one or two semesters of woodshop were considered trained and ready to take jobs in this field; but in art, six to eight semesters of work were required. Other courses, in the commercial and industrial fields, required a minimum of three or four semesters of study before the training was considered on a level with genuine vocational training.

It was therefore possible to measure the results of regular high-school vocational training in Seattle, and to compare them with the results of Smith-Hughes training in the same city. The records of the Seattle high schools were carefully checked to make sure that all youth classed as vocationally trained had fulfilled the minimum requirements set by the school officials. The same criteria of relationship between job and training were used as had been used in the case of Smith-Hughes trained youth.

Of all Seattle youth who were interviewed in the survey of youth in the labor market, 1,178 or 27 percent had completed one vocational course or more of study in the regular high schools. (This figure did not include many other youth who had taken one semester or more of high-school vocational work but who had not completed the minimum requirements for completion of the various courses.)

Labor-Market Status of Youth

Four out of every ten youth trained in the regular high schools were young men. Nine out of ten had entered the labor market at some time, and seven of these were still working or seeking work at the time of the survey. This was a higher proportion than was found in any of the other groups in Seattle—the Smith-Hughes trained youth, those trained in private vocational schools, or those with no recorded training of a vocational nature.

The proportion of labor-market youth who were employed at the time of the survey was higher in the regular high-school group than in the Smith-Hughes trained group. The comparatively short length of time spent in the labor market by Smith-Hughes youth—an average (mean) of 25 months, compared with 32 months for all other Seattle youth—probably explains this fact. Graduates of vocational programs in the regular high schools had less employment than graduates of private vocational schools (which catered to an older, more mature group of youth).

Of every 100 Seattle youth in the labor market on July 1, 1938, who had:	The number employed was:	The number employed full time was:
Regular high-school vocational training_____	83	71
Smith-Hughes training_____	78	67
Private school vocational training_____	88	78
No training of a vocational nature_____	82	69

Such small advantages in terms of employment as may have been derived from vocational training in the regular high schools, as opposed to no recorded vocational training of any sort, were entirely among the young women; male youth with regular high-school vocational training had no more employment than those with no training.

Employment in Field of Training

Of the 1,178 Seattle youth who had completed one vocational course or more in the regular high schools, and who subsequently entered the labor market, about half had obtained employment in which they were able to use the training they had received. About three-eighths had worked in jobs directly related to their training. (See appendix table 37.)

Of every 100 Seattle labor-market youth with vocational training in the regular high schools:

   37 had had jobs directly related to their training;
   14 had had jobs with an indirect relationship only;
   43 had had only jobs with no relationship to their training; and
   6 had had no jobs of 15 hours or more per week.

Fewer of these regular high-school trainees had had related jobs than had Seattle youth with Smith-Hughes training; but also fewer of them had had no jobs of 15 hours or more per week.[1]

Even when the high-school youth had completed two vocational courses or more in the regular high schools, as one in five did, their chances of obtaining work related to any of their training courses were not materially increased. Only 40 percent of such youth had obtained jobs directly related to any of the types of training they had acquired.

---

[1] See appendix table 26 for detailed figures. The large proportion of Seattle Smith-Hughes youth who had never held a full-time job was understandable in the light of the fact that 32 percent of this group had been in the labor market less than a year, as compared with only 19 percent of all other Seattle youth.

It should be remembered that all youth included in the group with regular high-school vocational training had completed their training courses, according to the specifications established by Seattle school authorities. Completed high-school vocational training probably represented a level of training more closely comparable, on the average, to uncompleted than to completed Smith-Hughes training.[2] When a comparison is made on this basis, the youth trained in regular high-school courses are placed in a more favorable light.

Of every 100 Seattle labor-market entrants who had received:	The number who had held related jobs was:
Regular high-school vocational training	51
Uncompleted Smith-Hughes training	40
Completed Smith-Hughes training	78

Eliminating from each group youth who had held no jobs of 15 hours or more per week, there was little difference between Seattle youth with uncompleted Smith-Hughes training and youth who completed their regular high-school training, in terms of the proportions obtaining related employment. Just over half of the remaining youth in each group had held jobs that were associated in some degree with their training.

The most successful vocational courses in Seattle's regular high schools were clerical in nature—notably retail selling and general clerking.

Of every 100 Seattle labor-market entrants with regular high-school training in:	The number who had held jobs directly related to their training was:
Retail selling	*70
General clerking	49
Stenography	44
Bookkeeping and stenography	*40
Bookkeeping	*39
Metal shop	32
Metal and wood shop	32
Bookkeeping and general clerking	*28
Woodshop	13
Drafting	*10
Art	8

* More than 25 but less than 50 youth.

It is particularly noteworthy that youth trained in retail selling, which required only one or two semesters of training, obtained related jobs in a large majority of cases, while youth trained in art, which required the longest training period—six to eight semesters of study—

---

[2] Uncompleted Smith-Hughes training, it will be remembered, was defined as at least one semester of full-time Smith-Hughes work, but not enough to enable the student to graduate from the program. This degree of training was comparable to completed training in the regular high schools, in terms of average number of semester hours spent in vocational courses.

had related employment in the smallest proportion of cases. The fact that some programs are of longer duration than others, then, does not necessarily mean that these programs are more likely to be of assistance to youth in finding appropriate jobs.

Apparently high-school vocational courses had some value for youth who intended to go into clerical work; but if they desired to enter the trades and industries, or the arts, they could expect little in the way of adequate preparation in the regular high schools. In the industrial field the vocational programs given at Edison School under the Smith-Hughes system produced much better results, in general, than the high-school programs, although the number of Seattle youth interviewed who had studied in individual Smith-Hughes industrial programs was too small to allow precise statistical comparisons to be made.

The only individual program at Edison School which was roughly comparable to certain of the vocational programs in the regular high schools, and which had more than 50 registrants, was the business training program. The various high-school commercial programs are here compared with completed and uncompleted Smith-Hughes business training, in terms of the percent of youth who found jobs that were directly related to their training.

Of every 100 Seattle labor-market entrants with:	The number who had held jobs directly related to their training was:
Smith-Hughes business training:	
Complete	*65
Incomplete	*39
Regular high-school training in:	
Retail selling	*70
General clerking	49
Stenography	44
Bookkeeping	*39

* More than 25 but less than 50 youth.

Of the regular high-school courses, only retail selling resulted in a degree of employment in field of training comparable to that attained by youth who had completed their Smith-Hughes training. This is explained by several factors: the large demand for retail store salespersons, especially during the Christmas rush and at other busy seasons; the selective policy pursued by the regular high schools in filling classes in retailing; and the efficient relationship worked out jointly by the schools and the large stores in Seattle for placing the youth once they were trained.

Youth in the other regular high-school commercial courses, particularly general clerking and stenography, fell below the Edison youth with completed business training in securing related employment. They compared favorably, however, with the Edison youth who had not completed their training. Apparently in these cases completed training in regular high school was at least equivalent to uncompleted Smith-Hughes business training in terms of enabling youthful labor-market entrants to secure appropriate jobs.

Duration of Jobs and Earnings

The full-time jobs of youth trained in the regular high schools of Seattle averaged 3.7 months in duration. Jobs in their fields of training lasted 5 months on the average, and jobs with no relationship to training lasted only 3 months. These figures were the same as those for Smith-Hughes youth in Seattle.

Average earnings of Seattle youth with regular high-school vocational training amounted to $18.90 per week for full-time work at the time of the survey. This was a dollar more than the average for Smith-Hughes youth (two-thirds of whom were girls), but less than the average for those with no training of a vocational sort. (The latter group included an especially large number of university-trained youth in Seattle.)

Among Seattle youth with full-time jobs on July 1, 1938, who had:	Average weekly earnings were:
Regular high-school vocational training	$18. 90
Smith-Hughes vocational training	17. 90
Private vocational training	18. 60
No training of a vocational nature	20. 10

On all full-time jobs they had held, Seattle youth with regular high-school training earned an average of $16.40 per week. On one full-time job in every eight they earned less than $10 per week. About one-fourth of all jobs paid more than $20 per week, but only 1 in 20 paid $35 or more. A majority of the jobs (60 percent) paid from $10 to $20 weekly.

There were sharp differences in average earnings of youth trained in the various high-school training programs. (See appendix table 38.) Highest earnings were those of youth with training in metal shop and in drafting.

Among Seattle youth with regular high-school training in:	Average weekly earnings on all full-time jobs were:
Metal shop	$20. 00
Drafting	*20. 00
Metal and woodshop	19. 60
Woodshop	19. 60
Bookkeeping and general clerking	*17. 70
Bookkeeping	16. 50
Art	15. 40
Bookkeeping and stenography	*15. 20
Retail selling	*15. 10
General clerking	14. 90
Stenography	14. 90

* More than 25 but less than 50 youth.

Several facts stand out from these figures. First, industrially trained youth had consistently higher earnings than youth with commercial training, as was the case in the Smith-Hughes group, in spite of the fact that they had had related employment in a smaller proportion of cases. Again, this was largely a reflection of the sex differential in earnings; the industrially trained youth were all young men.

The comparatively small earnings of commercially trained high-school youth and the high proportion of such youth who had had work in their fields of training are particularly notable in the case of the youth trained in retail selling; more than two-thirds of these youth had had jobs in their fields of training, but their earnings were among the lowest in the regular high-school group. As in the case of Smith-Hughes training, the programs which were most successful in helping youth to get jobs appropriate to their training apparently tended to be in fields where wages were relatively low.

Finally, it should be noted that in the only type of training where it was possible to compare Smith-Hughes and regular high-school trained youth—commercial training—the latter group proved to have a consistent advantage in earning power. The youth with business training at Edison Vocational School earned an average of only $14.70 per week on all full-time jobs, while the earnings of graduates from the commercial courses in the regular high schools ranged from $17.70 for those trained in both bookkeeping and general clerking down to $14.90 for those with stenographic training. The regular high-school trainees included only a slightly smaller proportion of girls than the Smith-Hughes group. Whether the composition of the two groups was different in other respects, whether there was a difference in the quality of the training, or whether other factors were at work, could not be determined from the data at hand.

Conclusions

Youth who received vocational training in the regular high schools were less successful than Smith-Hughes trained youth in getting jobs on which they were able to utilize their training; but they had at least as much total employment as did Smith-Hughes trainees, and their earnings were higher than those of the Smith-Hughes trained youth. Commercial students in the regular high schools were more successful than industrial students in obtaining jobs related to their training, as was the case among Smith-Hughes trained youth, in spite of the prevalent notion that there is an oversupply of labor available in the clerical occupations. It must, of course, be kept in mind that the comparison of the two types of training was limited to Seattle, and therefore does not permit conclusions as to the relative merits of Smith-Hughes and other public school training programs elsewhere.[3]

VOCATIONAL TRAINING IN PRIVATE SCHOOLS

The private vocational schools which were available to youth in the four cities studied were many and varied. In all of the cities business training schools had a larger number of registrants than any other type of private school. Other sorts of schools which were found in every city were beauty schools, barber "colleges," nursing schools, and arts schools. Two of the four cities had YMCA-sponsored schools for business and technical students. Three had large colleges or universities which offered professional courses.

St. Louis, the largest city studied here, had the greatest number and variety of private vocational schools. They included schools of advertising, aviation, brewing, chiropractic science, dressmaking, embalming, insurance, laboratory technique, massage, music, pharmacy, and welding. In addition there was a privately operated trade school with such courses as air conditioning, auto-repair work, carpentry, drafting, electricity, machine shop, painting, patternmaking, plumbing, power-plant operation, and refrigeration. Many of these subjects duplicated programs offered in the St. Louis public schools.

Only a small number of the youth classed as having completed private vocational school were trained in professional types of work. A very few of the oldest youth (the 1929 eighth-grade class) may have completed college courses in accounting, social work, education, or similar subjects. These would have been included in the sample studied, but could not have been numerous enough to affect the results very much. Most of the youth who were in training for the more advanced professions, such as law, medicine, teaching, and research had not yet completed their training at the time of the survey.

It is difficult to determine the relative efficiency of private training schools, or types of schools, in placing youth in jobs. Many business colleges claimed practically 100-percent placement of their students.

---

[3] The following statement by a St. Louis girl suggests that the situation there may have been somewhat similar to that in Seattle with respect to the greater effectiveness of completed Smith-Hughes training in enabling youth to get related jobs:

"If you're going into the business world, I think Hadley is much better than high school. We get much more real training at Hadley. When girls get out of high school they can take only about 80 words a minute in shorthand, where we take 120 to 140 words. We can type about 20 words a minute faster than they can, too. And then we take much more bookkeeping and extra courses like comptometer operation . . . Some people go to Hadley because they think it's easier, but it's not. We work much harder than they do in high school because at Hadley you have to have an average of 80 percent in all your subjects before you can graduate, while in high school you just have to get a passing grade."

In some cases the records bore this out; but the claims made by proprietors of other schools were sometimes exaggerated, as indicated by the following statement of a Birmingham girl who had graduated from a business college:

> Of course the head of the school told me he couldn't absolutely guarantee that I'd get a job, but he told me he could say that in all the years he'd been running that school no girl had ever left without a job. Well, that was just a story. In the 4 months I was there, only four girls got jobs, and two of them had to find their own jobs. Some girls who have finished their courses practically live at the school, waiting for jobs. Every time the telephone rings, everybody jumps.

In a few instances training had little relation to the state of the labor market. In one of the cities studied there was a school devoted exclusively to Diesel engineering. The expansion of Diesel-engine work had been greatly exaggerated by this school in numerous advertisements, and the fact that most jobs operating Diesel engines are held by persons with experience in gasoline-engine work was ignored. In the summer of 1938 more than 50 students were paying a minimum tuition of $230 for a 3-month course in this school, in spite of the fact that very few of them could have been expected to get jobs in Diesel work.

Several other types of private vocational schools have misrepresented the extent of labor-market opportunities in various cities. Air-conditioning schools advertise widely that there are great opportunities in this field, in spite of the fact that plumbers and sheet-metal workers are employed as a rule to install air-conditioning units. Other types of schools which have been found to be inaccurate in their representation of job openings include "embalming" schools and "civil service" schools.[4]

In some places there is State regulation of private courses in nursing and of beauty and barber schools, to insure certain minimum standards of instruction and of efficiency at graduation. In most fields, however, there is no such regulation to hinder the less scrupulous school proprietors from misrepresenting the state of the labor market, the quality of the instruction offered, and the probability of placement. Regulation of private schools is clearly needed, not only in the interest of youth, but also in the interest of the great majority of private vocational schools which operate honestly and efficiently.

Who Attended Private Schools

Of the youth who had no vocational training within the framework of the public school system, about one in every nine had completed

---

[4] See Marshall, Thomas O. and Fleming, Ralph D., "Gyp Training Schools," *Occupations*, Vol. XVII, No. 3, December 1938, pp. 197–203.

training programs in private vocational schools.[5] The figures for the four cities were as follows:

Of every 100 youth who had no vocational training in the public schools in:	The number who had completed vocational programs in private schools was:
St. Louis	14
Birmingham	6
Denver	12
Seattle	7

A much larger proportion of youth had completed vocational programs in private schools than had entered programs in Smith-Hughes schools in every city except St. Louis, where because of the well-developed system of federally aided training the Smith-Hughes registrants were about equal in number to the private school graduates. In Seattle the graduates of private vocational schools were far out-numbered by the vocational graduates of the regular high schools, but were twice as numerous as the Smith-Hughes registrants.

The privately trained group was, on the average, slightly older and more mature than the Smith-Hughes group. Almost three-fourths of the private school graduates were young women, most of whom had had commercial training in business colleges. Seattle and Denver had the largest proportion of women among private school youth, and St. Louis the smallest.

Of every 100 youth trained in private vocational schools in:	The number of females was:
St. Louis	65
Birmingham	77
Denver	78
Seattle	78

These figures represent a higher proportion of young women than obtained among Smith-Hughes trained youth in any of the cities or among youth trained in the regular high schools of Seattle.

Once they had completed their training programs, nine-tenths of the youth from private vocational schools entered the labor market at some time or other. Almost three-fourths were still in the labor force at the time of the survey. These figures are above the average for all youth, although somewhat lower than the corresponding figures for Smith-Hughes youth.

Employment

In each of the four cities surveyed, youth with vocational training in private schools had more employment at the time of the survey

---

[5] Youth with vocational training in the public schools are excluded here because an undetermined number of them had had private vocational school training in addition to their public school courses.

than youth with Smith-Hughes training or no training of a vocational nature. Only in Birmingham and Seattle, however, was private school training significantly more productive of employment than Smith-Hughes training.

Among labor-market youth in:	Of every 100 with private vocational school training, the number employed on July 1, 1938, was:	Of every 100 with Smith-Hughes training, the number employed on July 1, 1938, was:
St. Louis	86	83
Birmingham	85	76
Denver	89	88
Seattle	88	78

Taking the four cities together, vocational training in the private schools appeared to be demonstrably more effective in terms of employment than Smith-Hughes training. And when youth with private vocational school training were compared with youth having no training of any sort, they showed from 1 to 10 percent more employment, and a third less unemployment, than the completely untrained group.

All of the privately trained youth included in this study had completed their training programs, as was the case with the youth who had had regular high-school training of a vocational nature in Seattle. But this did not explain the difference in employment status between youth trained in private and public vocational schools, since youth trained in private schools had more employment than those with completed training in the regular high schools in Seattle and more than youth with completed Smith-Hughes training in each of the cities except Denver, where the group with completed Smith-Hughes training was too small for the difference to be statistically significant.

Earnings

Average earnings of youth trained in private vocational schools, on jobs they were holding at the time of the survey, amounted to $16.70 per week in the four cities. This was almost exactly the same as the average for youth who had no recorded training whatsoever. The relative earning power of private school and Smith-Hughes trainees varied from city to city.

Among youth working at full-time jobs on July 1, 1938, in:	Average weekly earnings of those with private vocational school training were:	Average weekly earnings of those with Smith-Hughes training were:
St. Louis	$16.50	$16.00
Birmingham	16.90	18.20
Denver	16.20	18.90
Seattle	18.60	17.90

It should be remembered that the earnings of the Smith-Hughes youth in Birmingham were relatively high mainly because this group included only white youth, and that the high earnings of the Smith-Hughes group in Denver were those of male youth only. In St. Louis and Seattle privately trained youth earned more than Smith-Hughes trained youth in spite of the fact that the first-named group included a higher proportion of girls in both cities.

There was a slight tendency for the youth with private school training to advance to jobs with higher wages more frequently than other youth. Taking the cities together:

Of every 100 shifts in job or wage status experienced by youth with:	The number resulting in increased earnings was:	The number resulting in decreased earnings was:
Private vocational training	64	22
Smith-Hughes training	61	25
No training of a vocational nature	60	28

Unfortunately, detailed information was not obtained regarding the type of training acquired by each youth in private vocational school, so individual work histories could not be analyzed in the light of the training received. In general, however, it may be said that private vocational schools were more successful than public schools in enabling youth to get jobs, though corresponding benefits in wages were not consistently in evidence.

There are several probable reasons for the apparent superiority of the private vocational schools over public schools in sending youth into employment. First, the private schools tend to attract a selected group of youth, who know what they want and who are serious enough and prosperous enough to pay tuition for their training. Many of these youth are high-school graduates who have gone to business college or other private schools after some experience in the labor market. While this is also true of many youth trained in the Smith-Hughes schools, the youth with private-school training are on the average an older, more experienced group. One Birmingham business college reported that the average educational level of its students upon entrance was 1 year of college.

Second, private vocational schools often have more up-to-date equipment than the public schools. They operate on a competitive basis, so that they must make their programs as modern and efficient as possible in order to attract students. In addition, the tuition fees they collect make it possible for them to spend more for equipment than many public schools which operate on small budgets.

Finally, the placement services of the private vocational schools are in many cases more closely keyed to the labor market than those of the public schools. Schools for beauty operators, for example, are often run in conjunction with beauty parlors, and students are accepted only as fast as is warranted by the need for trained operators. Officials of beauty schools questioned in several of the cities claimed 90- to 100-percent placement. The private schools are highly motivated to develop efficient methods of placing students, since their very existence often depends on their ability to show results in return for the money expended by their students on tuition.

Conclusions

The figures presented in the foregoing section do not necessarily mean that private schools are inherently superior to public schools in fitting youth for jobs. They do suggest that the public schools could be improved with regard to equipment, instruction, and placement services. Differences in effectiveness which may be due to the fact that a more advanced and serious group of students attend the private schools, however, will probably persist.

Chapter VI

GUIDANCE, PLACEMENT, AND ATTITUDES OF TRAINED YOUTH

VOCATIONAL EDUCATION entails more than training in the classroom and shop. Quite as important as the training program itself is what comes before and after: vocational guidance, to steer youth into lines of study and work for which they are best fitted and in which there are job opportunities; and vocational placement, to help youth find jobs in their fields of training when they leave school. The best of vocational schools can do little to help youth unless they get the right human material with which to work, and unless they are in constant and close touch with the labor market so that trained youth can be placed in jobs. All three sectors of the field of vocational education—guidance, training, and placement—must be developed together and closely coordinated with each other if a maximum of benefit is to be derived by youth from their training.

In preceding chapters vocational training programs have been discussed in some detail. Vocational guidance and placement, however, have been touched on only incidentally. It is the purpose of this chapter to discuss briefly these remaining aspects of vocational education, and to analyze the attitudes of youth toward the training they have undergone.

VOCATIONAL GUIDANCE

Only one Smith-Hughes trained youth in six, in the four cities, reported having received in the public school system any advice or guidance which led him to enter vocational school.[1] This ratio held

---

[1] The New York State Board of Regents' Inquiry similarly found that of male vocational school graduates, 24 percent had received some vocational guidance, but only 8 percent had been helped in this way in the public schools. (Norton, Thomas L., *Education for Work*, The Regents' Inquiry Into the Character and Cost of Public Education in the State of New York, New York: The McGraw-Hill Book Co., Inc., 1938, p. 27.)

approximately true in St. Louis, Birmingham, and Denver. In Seattle twice as large a proportion—a third of the trained youth—had received guidance. Slightly more of the unemployed group (18 percent) than of the employed group (16 percent) in the four cities had received guidance before entering their training programs.

The reasons for the failure of vocational guidance to reach the great majority of youth lie in the newness of the movement for individual guidance and in the shortage of trained counselors in the schools. All of the cities had some provision for guidance in their secondary schools, but in nearly every school the work fell on the shoulders of one or two members of the teaching staff as an extra duty or, at best, as a part-time responsibility.

In St. Louis the Division of Vocational Counseling, with three full-time counselors, was established in 1925; but this meager provision for a city of nearly a million population was discontinued 10 years later, at the depth of the depression, because of its cost. Thereafter the duty of advising students in choosing occupations fell to the principals and vocational teachers of the various schools. Under these circumstances no systematic approach to the guidance problem was possible. The following comment by a St. Louis youth was fairly typical:

> When I was in high school there just didn't seem to be anyone who could take time to help me decide what I wanted to do. There ought to be more vocational guidance in the schools. They ask you what you want to take, but how does a 12-year-old boy know what he wants to be? And then there are so many required subjects. They say, "Now you have to take this, and you have to take that; and you have one period left over. What do you want to take? If you want to be a doctor you should have Latin." How did I know whether I wanted to be a doctor or not? They ought to find out what kids can do best and then teach them to do that. Education ought to bring out what's already in kids, not try to put something new in them.

Birmingham's largest high school had two advisers for boys and one for girls. In the entire white secondary school system there were 13 advisers, all of whom combined this work with part-time teaching. These advisers tried to assemble vocational information, brought leading men in various fields to the schools to talk to selected groups of interested students, and arranged trips through factories and stores. But the number of advisers was so small that only a minority of youth received individual attention. There was no organized system of vocational guidance in the Negro schools.

In Denver and Seattle each junior and senior high school had a boys' adviser and a girls' adviser. In the former city the number of students per adviser was so large that only the exceptional youth—"geniuses" or "problem cases"—were likely to receive much individual attention. In Seattle the advisers had fewer students and were able to devote at least half of their time to guidance, with the result that about twice as many trained youth had received guidance there as was the case in any of the other cities. But in most of the schools in the four cities individual guidance was given only to youth who sought it; other youth had no personal contact with the advisers.

Many employers in the four cities criticized the failure of guidance programs to reach a majority of high-school youth. Typical were the remarks of a personnel official in a Birmingham department store:

> I am thoroughly in sympathy with vocational training, and I believe there is a great future for it. But in Birmingham it is still in its beginning stage. My chief criticism is that the school has not yet adopted a method whereby students can be selected for the courses according to their natural aptitudes. Every person does not have the natural qualifications to sell. . . . But the classes in retailing and salesmanship at the Paul Hayne School must accept anyone, regardless of his or her natural aptitude.

Numerous studies have shown that the great majority of youth desire to enter the professions or to do white-collar work of some sort. The New York State Regents' Inquiry found that a third of the high-school graduates of both sexes wanted professional jobs, and that another 37 percent of the boys and 57 percent of the girls wanted clerical, trade, or public-service jobs.[2] This is perhaps not unreasonable, since high-school graduates are a selected group to begin with, and a majority of them do go into clerical work or, eventually, into the professions.[3] A study of the occupational preferences of 1,230 high-school juniors and seniors in a Mobile, Ala., high school showed that 39 percent wanted professional work, 29 percent other white-collar work, and 32 percent skilled or semiskilled work. Only one individual desired domestic work, and none wished to work at unskilled labor,[4] which was hardly surprising.

The occupational preferences of youth do not always square, however, with the actual opportunities open to them. The Maryland study of the American Youth Commission showed that while two-thirds of the youth (urban and rural, and of all levels of education) preferred white-collar occupations, only a little over one-third actually obtained this type of employment. Over 38 percent wanted to do professional or technical work, but less than 8 percent were able to get such work.[5]

---

[2] Eckert, Ruth E. and Marshall, Thomas O., *When Youth Leave School*, The Regents' Inquiry Into the Character and Cost of Public Education in the State of New York, New York: The McGraw-Hill Book Co., Inc., 1938, p. 219. The proportions cited exclude those who did not specify their preferences.

[3] About two-thirds of all youth—54 percent of the males, 79 percent of the females—who had just 12 years of education in the seven cities covered by the larger youth survey actually went into white-collar work. (See Westefeld, Albert, *op. cit.*)

[4] Data from Mr. K. J. Clark, principal of Murphy High School, Mobile, Ala.

[5] Bell, Howard M., *Youth Tell Their Story*, Washington: American Council on Education, 1938, p. 132.

If youth had a knowledge of their own aptitudes, of the nature of various occupations, and of the opportunities available in different fields, they would be able to choose their vocations more intelligently than they can today. The majority of young people who choose their occupations do so on the basis of inexpert advice offered by parents or friends, or because of scraps of information or misinformation which have come their way. Actually, occupations are more frequently determined by chance than by choice; they depend largely on the jobs youth happen to find early in their employment careers.

The function of an effective guidance program is to narrow the gap between occupational preferences and actual realities—to encourage more youth to prepare for the types of jobs which they are likely to obtain. To accomplish this on a large scale it would be necessary to (1) sponsor educational assemblies and hold individual conferences which would explain the characteristics, advantages, and handicaps in each of the important occupations; (2) discourage or prevent youth from taking training for which they are not qualified; and (3) limit the number to be trained to the number likely to be absorbed in the labor market. Surveys of occupational opportunities would also need to be conducted in the various communities, and the results made known to teachers and students alike. Such studies, combined with the guidance program outlined above, would add immeasurably to the effectiveness of vocational training.

VOCATIONAL PLACEMENT

Of all jobs held by vocationally trained youth in the 4 cities, only 1 in 12 was obtained through the vocational schools. While the proportion of first jobs thus obtained was undoubtedly somewhat higher, this figure indicates that such placement services as there were in the schools where these youth received their training helped the youth to find jobs in only a small minority of cases.

Of every 100 jobs held at any time by youth in the 4 cities, the number located through:	Among youth with Smith-Hughes training was:	Among youth with no Smith-Hughes training was:
Friends	27	29
Personal applications	22	25
Previous employers	16	15
Relatives	14	16
Schools	8	4
Employment agencies	6	3
Want ads	4	3
Other means	3	5

Smith-Hughes trained youth located more jobs through schools and employment agencies, and consequently fewer through friends, relatives, and personal applications, than youth with no Smith-Hughes

"... *an effective guidance program narrows the gap between occupational preferences and actual realities* ..."

training.[6] As youth in both groups spent more and more time in the labor market, they tended to locate an increasing proportion of jobs through previous employers and a decreasing proportion of them through relatives and friends.

Often a youth would use one device after another to secure jobs, as exemplified by the statement of one Seattle youth:

After I got my certificate in auto mechanics in June '35, I looked for a job for several weeks, but "nothing doing." Then I saw an ad in the paper for a mechanic, and got the job. It paid $25 a week, but the trouble was it only lasted 2 weeks. After that I was out again, and no luck, so in the fall I went east of the mountains to pick apples. In November I came back to Seattle. The Edison School people got me a job putting into shape new cars that had been brought by caravan across the country for the auto show. But when the show opened in December, that was the end of that. By the following February I was getting pretty desperate. Then I remembered that I knew something about the care of trees from my high-school years, when I used to help my brother, who did that sort of work. So I had a brain storm and put an ad in the paper for work pruning and spraying trees. A landscape gardening company answered the ad, and put me on as a general laborer. I've been there ever since.

Of course, I want to get back into my own line of work—auto-repair work— but there aren't many jobs open and the union has most of them sewed up. I guess that's all right; the union has to look after its unemployed members. But I think Edison should make some arrangement with the union to have its graduates go right into union apprenticeships, so their training won't be wasted. Anyway, I'm keeping my hand in by doing auto-repair jobs for my friends on Saturdays and Sundays. And I know a fellow who runs a garage, and he says he'll give me a regular mechanic's job as soon as business picks up a little more.

The low proportion of job placements through the schools was partly a reflection of the fact that none of the vocational schools covered by this survey in the four cities had adequate placement services. In Denver the Emily Griffith Opportunity School, where part-time evening and extension students received Smith-Hughes training, had a placement service, and this was available to youth from all public and parochial schools who cared to register there. West High School, where the day-training programs covered by this survey were given, however, had no placement service of its own. In the other three cities such placements as were made through the vocational schools were the work of individual instructors, some of whom maintained close contact with the labor market in their special fields.

In each of the cities there was some provision for placing out-of-school youth through junior divisions of the State Employment

[6] The New York State Board of Regents' Inquiry found that only about 7 percent of all high-school graduates and 3 percent of those who failed to graduate, had been directed to their jobs by their schools. Less than 1 percent had found their jobs through government placement agencies. (Spaulding, Francis T., *High School and Life.* The Regents' Inquiry Into the Character and Cost of Public Education in the State of New York, New York: The McGraw-Hill Book Co., Inc., 1938, p. 61.)

Services, and the vocational schools maintained a close relationship with these agencies. In Denver the National Youth Administration contributed workers to the staff of the Junior Division of the Colorado State Employment Service, and in St. Louis the Board of Education furnished several interviewing counselors to the Junior Division of the Missouri State Employment Service to aid in placing vocational students and other youth. Supplementary placement work was done by the vocational school in the latter city, but according to one youth:

> The Hadley employment service has its advantages but its disadvantages too. For one thing, employers in St. Louis depend on Hadley and don't do much training in the factories. The factories use the school as an employment agency because they know that boys just out of school will work for lower wages; most of them have no dependents, and a good many of them don't even have to be independent while they're living at home.

Seattle had a Public Schools Placement Bureau from 1919 until 1938, when it became the Junior Employment and Counseling Service, affiliated with the Washington State Employment Service. The Seattle agency was the joint project of the Seattle School Board, which furnished the quarters and equipment and paid the salaries of two senior staff members; the State Department of Social Security, which furnished other staff members and supervised the agency; the State Employment Service, which furnished the forms used and cooperated in other ways; and the NYA, which furnished some clerical assistance. This type of cooperative arrangement was considered by local officials to be very useful in keeping the schools in close touch with the various government services and with the labor market. Out of 4,170 youth who were registered in the Seattle agency during the year 1937–38, approximately one-fourth (1,065) were placed on jobs. But only 330 of these were sent to permanent, full-time jobs, so that only 1 out of every 12 registrants could have been considered as satisfactorily placed.

A survey made by the Children's Bureau of the United States Department of Labor at the end of 1936 showed that less than half of all cities with a population of 100,000 or more in 1930 had junior placement services in which one person or more devoted full time to the placement of young people. Less than 10 percent of the cities with a population of 25,000 to 100,000 and less than 1 percent of the cities under 10,000 had junior placement offices. In 1936 the number of placements made by junior placement officers in 67 cities was less than half as great as the number of new applicants; and about half of all placements lasted less than a month.[7] As junior placement agencies become more generally accepted and more adequately staffed,

---

[7] Palmer, Jane, *Junior Placement: A Survey of Junior-Placement Offices in Public Employment Centers and in Public School Systems of the United States*, Publication No. 256, Children's Bureau, U. S. Department of Labor, Washington, D. C., 1940, pp. 7, 12, 95.

the number of youth finding jobs through them may be expected to increase.

Difficulties in Securing Employment

The extremes of good and bad fortune in securing related employment are typified by the experiences of two St. Louis youth, both trained in the machine-shop program at Hadley Vocational School. One received his diploma on a Friday and went to work in a machine shop the following Monday; the other had been unemployed for months at a time, and had never been able to find a job in the type of work for which he had been trained. The latter youth described his difficulties as follows:

There just weren't enough jobs to go around in those days. I followed the papers and made the rounds, going from machine shop to metal shop to factory, but everywhere I went they wanted fellows with 5 or 6 years of experience and practical work behind them, or else someone who had specialized in one particular machine-shop operation. I finally got a job driving a truck.

More than a quarter of all youth with Smith-Hughes training reported encountering special difficulties in securing work.[8] The proportion of trained youth reporting such difficulties was only slightly lower than the corresponding proportion of untrained youth.

Of every 100 youth with:	The number reporting special difficulties in getting jobs was:
Completed Smith-Hughes training	27
Uncompleted Smith-Hughes training	30
No Smith-Hughes training	31

There were sharp differences among these groups in the types of difficulties most frequently encountered in the search for jobs. The Smith-Hughes trained youth who reported special difficulties, especially those with completed training, said that they had been handicapped by lack of experience more frequently, and by lack of general or specialized training less frequently, than other youth.

Of every 100 youth who reported special difficulties in securing jobs, the number whose chief difficulty was:	Among youth with completed Smith-Hughes training was:	Among youth with uncompleted Smith-Hughes training was:	Among youth with no Smith-Hughes training was:
Lack of experience	71	64	52
Lack of general training	7	10	10
Lack of specialized training	2	9	9
Insufficient education	2	4	6
Too young	3	4	5
"Lack of pull"	2	1	2
Physical defects	2	2	3
Union restrictions	1	2	4
Other difficulties	10	4	9

[8] "Special difficulties" are defined as obstacles to employment other than general labor-market conditions such as unemployment—difficulties arising from personal characteristics or specific situations which handicap youth in the labor market.

Youth with completed programs felt little need for more specialized training; but they were acutely aware of their lack of actual work experience, in spite of the practical shop or office work done in the Smith-Hughes schools. It may be assumed that they felt a greater need for experience because the work which they sought was more likely to be skilled or semiskilled than in the case of untrained youth, so that experience was more likely to be important.

Sometimes the need for actual work experience is so great that youth volunteer their services free in order to obtain practice in their chosen trades so that they can get paid jobs later on. One Birmingham girl reported as follows:

I went down to see a man who advertised for a bookkeeper, but right away he asked me what experience I'd had. I told him I was a graduate of the business training course at Paul Hayne School, but he said it would take him 2 weeks to teach me the job, and he had to find someone who could start right in. So I asked him if I couldn't just work there for nothing till I could say I'd had some experience. He just yelled at me and said that's why so many women are working for such low wages today; too many of them want to work for nothing or practically nothing and take jobs away from people with families who need the money. He said I'd never get paid, at least not much, once I started working for nothing. As soon as I'd start talking about getting paid, he said, they'd start talking about firing me. I guess he was right, but you have to get started somehow, and I needed a job too.

It cannot be concluded from the responses of the youth that shop or office practice should be emphasized at the expense of general training in the theoretical and social-economic fields. The fact that lack of general training was also frequently mentioned as a special difficulty in getting jobs suggests that such a policy would not solve the problem. But the extent to which inadequate experience was mentioned as a handicap indicates that Smith-Hughes training should concentrate as much attention as possible upon practical work, in office or shop, even though it be recognized that such experience cannot entirely take the place of experience on the job.

ATTITUDES OF YOUTH REGARDING VOCATIONAL TRAINING

In order to determine the attitudes of trained youth toward the Smith-Hughes programs in which they had been registered, and toward vocational training in general, a supplementary schedule or questionnaire was filled out for a representative cross section of trained youth. The replies to this questionnaire constituted an evaluation by youth of their own vocational training.

Assistance in Getting Jobs

The first question, asked only of youth who had had some employment since leaving school, was, "Did your vocational training assist you in getting a job?" A little over half (52 percent) of all youth queried on this point answered in the affirmative. (See appendix table 39.) The proportion of "yes" replies in the four cities was 75 percent among youth with completed training, 39 percent among those who did not complete their programs. These figures were similar to those obtained from an analysis of the actual work histories of the youth.[9]

The percent of youth reporting that their training had helped them in getting jobs in the following cities:	Among youth with completed training was:	Among youth with uncompleted training was:
St. Louis	75	40
Birmingham	58	31
Denver	*	25
Seattle	87	37

*Less than 25 youth.

In Seattle seven out of eight youth with completed training reported that their school programs had actually helped them to get work. St. Louis, with three out of four answering in the affirmative, had the next highest proportion. Birmingham and Denver youth reported less assistance, although well over half of the youth with completed training answered in the affirmative in the former city.

This statement by a St. Louis youth with training in architectural drafting illustrates how vocational training may help youth to get jobs:

When I graduated I went around to all the architects' offices but they didn't have any openings. The only job I could find for a while was in a hardware store. Then a friend of mine who works in a sash and door factory told me to apply for a job in the drafting department there. The employment manager said no more draftsmen were needed, but asked me if I knew anything about cabinetmaking. I'd only had about 5 weeks of woodworking at Hadley, but I said "yes," and they put me on. They promised to transfer me to the drafting department, and they did in about 6 months. Over there I designed kitchen cabinets. But I quit when work got slack and they asked me to report to the cabinet room again.

After I was out of work for a month, my cousin told me to apply at the refriger ator factory where he worked. They didn't need any draftsmen right then, either, but as soon as I told them I had done some sheet-metal work at Hadley (13 weeks of it), they put me on as a metal polisher. After 6 weeks they transferred me to the drafting room, where I still work.

There were large differences among youth who were employed full time at the time of interview and those who were employed only part time or completely unemployed, in terms of whether they thought their training had helped them to get jobs. The difference was further accentuated by completion of training. Almost four-fifths of all youth with completed training who were working at full-time jobs said that they had been benefited by their training in getting work, compared with less than a quarter of those with uncompleted training

[9] See p. 43.

who had only part-time work. Following were the responses of trained
youth who had held jobs at some time, according to their employment
status at the time of the survey:

Among trained youth who on July 1, 1938 were:	The percent stating that they had been helped in getting jobs by their training was:	
	With completed training:	With uncompleted training:
Employed full time	78	42
Employed part time	47	23
Unemployed	68	32

More young women than young men among those who had had
some employment had found their training to be of some value in
obtaining jobs.

The percent of youth reporting that their training had helped them to get jobs in the following cities:	Among young men was:	Among young women was:
St. Louis	46	56
Birmingham	42	*
Denver	29	—
Seattle	63	66

* Less than 25 youth.

The racial factor also showed up clearly in the responses to this
question. In St. Louis well over half of all white youth said that
they had used their training in getting jobs, as compared with only 40
percent of the Negro youth interviewed.

In St. Louis it was also possible to break down the responses by
types of training. There were small differences among youth trained
in various programs, as shown by the following table:

Among St. Louis youth trained in:	The percent reporting that their training had helped them to get jobs was:	
	With completed training:	With uncompleted training:
Commercial programs	76	46
Industrial programs	77	35
Women's programs	73	30
Arts programs	71	43

Again, these figures were essentially similar to those derived from
the analysis of actual jobs, as shown in the work histories of youth
in relation to training. The main difference was that youth with
uncompleted training reported a little less actual assistance in getting
jobs than their employment records indicated they might have
received.

As suggested by the analysis of work histories in chapter IV,
commercial programs in general, and the more specialized ones in
particular, were of the greatest amount of assistance in enabling youth
to get jobs, according to the youth themselves. Nine out of ten youth

with completed stenographic training said that it had helped them to find jobs. In every program youth with completed training reported more assistance in getting jobs than did youth with uncompleted training. This was particularly true in the case of industrially trained youth. Considering only youth with completed training, the young men with industrial training reported slightly more assistance from their vocational work in getting jobs than did those with commercial training.

It should be kept in mind that the sex composition of the groups in the different types of programs varied greatly. The difference between the commercial and industrial groups in amount of assistance reported closely parallels the differential in the responses of the young men and women.

Assistance on the Job

A considerable majority of St. Louis youth who had held one job or more reported that their training had been of some assistance to them in working on the job. Six out of every ten trained youth in that city—eight-tenths of those with completed training, and over half of those who failed to complete their programs—replied in the affirmative to the question, "Has your vocational training been of any help to you in working on the job in any employment you have had?"

The percent of trained youth reporting that their vocational training had helped them on the job in:	With completed training was:	With uncompleted training was:
St. Louis	80	51
Birmingham	78	57
Denver	*	48
Seattle	91	54

*Less than 25 youth.

Seattle youth again reported greater benefits from their training, on the average, than did youth in the other cities. Both Denver and Birmingham youth reported much more assistance received from their training once they were on the job than they had received in getting employment. The same was true, although the difference was somewhat smaller, in the other two cities.

The margin between youth with completed and those with uncompleted training, in terms of proportions reporting assistance on the job, was very wide in every city. Employment status at the time of the survey was also associated with sharp differences in response to this, as well as to the previous, question. Over four-fifths of all youth with completed training who were employed full-time reported that they had been assisted on the job, compared with less than a third of those whose training was incomplete and who were employed only part time.

Among trained youth who on July 1, 1938, were:	The percent stating that they had been helped on the job by their training was:	
	Among youth with completed training:	Among youth with uncompleted training:
Employed full time	83	55
Employed part time	56	32
Unemployed	73	39

As might be expected from their responses to the question regarding assistance in getting jobs, more young women than young men reported assistance on the job from their training programs in St. Louis. In Seattle, however, there was practically no difference between the sexes.

The percent of trained youth reporting that vocational training had helped them on the job in:	Among young men was:	Among young women was:
St. Louis	55	63
Birmingham	62	*
Denver	52	—
Seattle	75	74

*Less than 25 youth.

There was a large difference between races in St. Louis, with 61 percent of the whites but only 43 percent of the Negroes reporting that their training had assisted them on the job.

With respect to the various types of programs, more commercially trained youth in St. Louis reported that they had been assisted on the job by their vocational training than did youth with other sorts of training.

Among St. Louis youth trained in:	The percent reporting that vocational training had helped them on the job was:	
	With completed training:	With uncompleted training
Commercial programs	81	54
Industrial programs	80	48
Women's programs	78	38
Arts programs	62	46

A very high proportion of youth with completed training in cosmetology and stenography reported that vocational training had helped them on the job. In these two groups, as well as among former students of electricity, over nine-tenths of all youth who had finished their programs said that their training had been of some assistance in their work. The proportions of youth thus helped by the various types of programs were similar to the proportions whose work histories contained employment with some relationship to their training.

Thus, from the responses of the youth questioned as to whether their vocational education had been of assistance to them in getting jobs and in working on the job it is apparent that a majority of youth felt that the time they had spent in vocational school had not been wasted.

Criticisms of Programs

When questioned as to whether they wished to express any criticisms of vocational training as they had experienced it, only a minority of youth had specific criticisms to offer. (See appendix table 40.) Less than a fourth of all youth, whether employed in their fields of training, employed in other types of work, or unemployed, expressed definite opinions as to what was wrong with vocational training or how it could be improved. The other three-fourths either said that they had found their training worth while or could not formulate any definite criticism of it.

Of every 100 trained labor-market youth in the 4 cities,
> 48 said, "It was worth while;"
> 30 offered no criticism; and
> 22 offered definite criticisms.

It should be understood that many of the youth who offered no criticism may have been apathetic, rather than favorable, toward their vocational training; and that some of those who offered definite criticisms felt that in general the program was worth while in spite of certain shortcomings. Most of the youth felt that vocational school compared very favorably with the nonvocational high schools. According to one St. Louis boy who had studied to be a machinist at the Hadley Vocational School:

A high-school education alone doesn't mean very much. I know boys who have looked for jobs in downtown restaurants, and they found that even the dishwashers in the cafeterias have to be high-school graduates. The same thing is true of a lot of the unskilled work in the factories. So I don't think a high-school diploma is much of an advantage, unless, of course, you can't get a job at all without one. High-school graduates don't even know where to begin to look for jobs. But if you have a trade and know what kind of a job you can do, you can just take a telephone directory, list the names and addresses of all the plants that do that kind of work, and then begin looking for a job.

If you go to Hadley you are expected to work hard and take your work seriously; in order to get a diploma you have to make an average of G—Good—not only in the trade courses but in the classroom courses, too. Some of the boys who flunk some of the classroom work are allowed to finish their shop work, but they aren't given diplomas—just slips stating that they have completed so many hours of shop work.

The first year they circulate you through all the departments—woodwork, electricity, machine shop, and so on—and by the end of the year you're expected to know what you want to do. They give you some vocational counseling, too. Of course, they don't tell anyone that he can't take a certain course, but they tell you if they think you aren't fitted for the trade you choose. The Hadley Vocational School is a credit to St. Louis, and a boon to the people who can't afford to send their children to college but want them to have skilled trades . . . The standard of qualifications for the Hadley teachers is very high, too. In addition to being college graduates, they have to have 10 years of actual experience in their trades.

Birmingham and Denver youth gave the largest proportion of critical responses in evaluating their training, and St. Louis and Seattle the smallest proportion.

	The number expressing definite criticisms of their vocational
Of every 100 trained labor-market youth in:	*training was:*
St. Louis	21
Birmingham	35
Denver	49
Seattle	26

Taking the four cities together, more of the youth with uncompleted than of those with completed training—24 percent as compared with 19 percent—offered criticisms of their training. The most common criticism was that the training programs were not adequate. Youth with completed training voiced this criticism more frequently than those whose training was incomplete, indicating that after they had found jobs they felt a need for more specific types of training and longer programs.

Among youth who offered definite criticisms of their training programs:	*Was mentioned by this percent of youth with completed training:*	*Was mentioned by this percent of youth with uncompleted training:*
Incompleteness	24	13
Lack of equipment	8	13
Too much theory	6	8
Too low standards	6	4
Lack of teachers	3	5
Too short programs	4	2
Miscellaneous criticism	49	55

The large size of the "miscellaneous" group was due to the fact that many criticisms were either vague and general in nature or concerned with particular aspects of specific programs, so that they could not easily be classified under the general headings cited above.

The comments of one Birmingham youth trained in machine shop are representative of the criticisms of many youth who felt that their training had been incomplete:

I thought the course was pretty well rounded when I was in school, but since I got out I've learned that a fellow can't become a full-fledged machinist in 2 years. At the end of the course he can look for a job as a helper or an apprentice, but there aren't many of those jobs in Birmingham. If a fellow does get on as an apprentice, his 2 years of training at school only reduce his apprenticeship by 8 months. Furthermore, the machine-shop equipment at school is inadequate. Boys who have worked on the 12- and 14-inch lathes at school are scared to death when they have to run a 25- or 32-inch lathe on a regular job. In school they work with little old tool bits and they wouldn't even know how to sharpen a good-sized tool bit. I know the school can't install every type of machine you have to operate on a job. But it seems like some kind of system where we could get practice in a real machine shop part of the time would help a lot.

Expansion of Vocational Training

In spite of the fact that a third of all trained youth reported that vocational training had not helped them in getting jobs or in working on the job, about 95 percent of them said that they were in favor of expanding the vocational training offered in the public school system.

Of every 100 youth trained in:	The number favoring expansion of vocational training was:
St. Louis	96
Birmingham	96
Denver	89
Seattle	95

Another questionnaire, filled out by 200 Seattle young people (a cross section of all Seattle youth interviewed, regardless of vocational training), showed that 85 percent favored the expansion of the training offered in the public schools of that city. The parents of these youth favored the expansion of training in 92 percent of all cases.

Every trained Negro youth questioned on this point in St. Louis favored expansion of the program in that city. More than 19 out of every 20 trained white youth in St. Louis and Birmingham also held this opinion, regardless of program or completion of training.

This overwhelming majority in favor of the expansion of vocational education is probably a reflection of two factors: (1) the belief that vocational training is the most effective means of equipping youth for jobs; and (2) the realization, particularly on the part of youth who have actually experienced vocational training, that present-day systems of vocational education are limited in scope, with regard to both specialization of training and variety of programs offered.

Plans for the Future

When questioned as to their future plans, three-fifths of all youth with Smith-Hughes training said that they intended to get jobs, retain or advance in their present jobs, or get better jobs. Trained youth were more concerned with their individual economic problems and less concerned with obtaining further education than were other youth.

Among youth in the 4 cities who were questioned as to their future plans:	Was mentioned by this percent with Smith-Hughes training:	Was mentioned by this percent with no Smith-Hughes training:
Continuance of education	18	29
Securing of employment	14	12
Retention of or advancement in present job	30	23
Securing better job	17	14
Entering business	4	3
Entering the civil service	1	2
Getting married	6	4
Continuance of household responsibilities	7	10
Other plans	3	3

Two-thirds of all trained youth who were unemployed were concerned primarily with getting jobs, while two-thirds of those who were employed were chiefly interested in retaining or advancing in their present jobs or in securing better jobs.

CONCLUSIONS

From the data presented in this chapter, it is apparent that, although few trained youth reported having received assistance in the form of guidance or placement in the schools, most of them reacted very favorably to the training programs they had taken. A majority stated that their programs had helped them in obtaining jobs and in working on the job. Only a minority expressed definite criticisms of the programs, and a great majority were in favor of expanding the facilities for vocational training in their cities.

Chapter VII

CONCLUSIONS

WHAT ARE the outstanding results of the present survey, and what conclusion can be drawn from them?

In the first place, youth without any Smith-Hughes training fared almost as well in terms of total employment and earnings as did trained youth. This suggests that nonvocational education had about as much value as vocational training for the youth interviewed in these four cities.

It must be recognized, however, that vocational education aims at fitting youth for specific types of jobs; if it accomplishes this to a satisfactory degree, it has achieved its primary purpose, even though the jobs for which some youth have been trained are relatively low in pay. The work histories of trained youth, as well as the testimony of the youth themselves, indicate that vocational training helped a majority of them to find and keep jobs. The proportion of youth who had held jobs related to their training ranged from 30 to 83 percent of those trained in various training programs. In every known instance more youth obtained jobs in the fields for which they were trained than would have been expected on a basis of chance.

On the other hand, vocational training failed to achieve its main purpose in a sizable minority of the cases covered by this study. Of youth who failed to complete their training, about half had never held a job related to their training. This was perhaps to be expected. But more surprising were the facts that a quarter of those who had completed their training programs had never had related work, and that less than three-fifths of the employed youth with completed training were working at jobs directly related to that training at the time of the survey. These facts indicate that vocational training failed to meet the needs of a large number of trained youth.

FACTORS INFLUENCING THE EFFECTIVENESS OF VOCATIONAL TRAINING

It would be too much to expect all youth with Smith-Hughes vocational training to graduate directly into related employment. A certain number of them are bound to find jobs in other fields—sometimes good jobs. In such cases their training is not necessarily wasted; many of them may find it useful in connection with work at home or in their avocations. Nevertheless when a large number of trained youth do not use their training on the job, some explanation is indicated. The reasons for such a phenomenon are important for any appraisal of vocational training.

Several factors may have contributed to the failure of a quarter to a half of all trained youth surveyed to profit by their training. One hypothesis might be that the youth who entered vocational school programs were inferior to other youth in social background and scholastic ability. There is considerable evidence from other surveys that this has been the case in some places. The present survey, however, showed that there was no significant difference between trained and untrained youth either in social status or in ability as students (as measured by age at eighth-grade graduation). This explanation may therefore be ruled out as an important factor in explaining the lack of relationship between training and employment among many trained youth.

A more likely hypothesis is that vocational training is less effective than might otherwise be the case because of the lack of opportunity for individual guidance in the public schools. Only one youth in six in the four cities reported having received any guidance prior to entering vocational school. The other five-sixths presumably drifted into their vocational programs without benefit of vocational counseling. Undoubtedly a more adequate system of guidance would have discouraged some of the youth who were least fitted for the types of training offered under the Smith-Hughes plan from entering vocational programs. Other youth might have been persuaded to change from one program to another so that their training would be more appropriate to their abilities and better adjusted to the needs of the labor market. It is essential that more individual guidance be available to all youth, and particularly to youth desiring to enter specialized vocational programs.

A third and perhaps the most obvious explanation for the partial failure of vocational training to meet the needs of youth might be that the quality and content of vocational training are not such as to turn out well-trained workers. This is a charge often made, both by employers and by labor unions. As far as quality of training was concerned, however, there was no indication from the present survey that this was an important shortcoming of the Smith-Hughes schools. In a few instances in the four cities, it is true, the equipment used was so outmoded that the skills learned by youth at school were of less practical value than they should have been in helping youth to get or hold jobs. Shop courses in one or two cities, particularly those available to Negroes, were criticized by several youth on this score. The budget limitations of the Smith-Hughes schools sometimes prevented the schools from obtaining the best shop machinery.[1] To correct such conditions, where they exist, funds should be available for the purchase of new equipment so that training may at all times parallel as closely as possible actual working techniques in the community.

There were some indications that the content of vocational instruction could be improved, both in scope and orientation. Even among youth with completed training by far the most common criticism of the Smith-Hughes programs was that they were incomplete. But only a fifth of all youth with completed training offered any criticisms whatever, and only a fourth of these—5 percent of all youth with completed training—mentioned the matter of incompleteness.

Nevertheless data from the work histories of the youth indicate that the most thorough and specific sorts of training were most effective. Youth with completed training were far more likely than those with uncompleted training, and youth with the most specialized types of training (particularly in the commercial programs) more likely than those with relatively unspecialized training, to obtain jobs related to their vocational programs.

A fourth possibility is that the number of youth trained in various occupations may have had little relationship to labor-market needs. The present survey does not indicate that any great surplus of youth was trained in most of the fields served by Smith-Hughes training programs. It was, however, impossible to make any precise comparison of the number of youth trained in various specific lines of work and the number of jobs available in the same fields on the basis of the present survey.

There was some evidence that the types of training offered in the Smith-Hughes schools did not always correspond closely with labor-market needs. One indication was the fact that there were wide

[1] In one city covered by the survey of youth in the labor market, but not included among the four studied here, the reverse of the tendency cited above was found. A new course in bakery work was of little benefit to its graduates because the machines installed were too new. An investigation showed that the bakeries in town all used older equipment, and probably would continue to use it for some years. A similar situation prevailed in woodworking, where knowledge of the operation of modern machinery was of little use to youth who went to work in old-fashioned cabinetmakers' shops. In these instances the training programs may have been a little too far in advance of labor-market conditions.

variations in the amounts of related employment obtained by youth in different programs. Other evidence took the form of complaints from labor unions that too many workers trained or partly trained in Smith-Hughes programs were entering certain lines of work, or complaints from employers that other occupations were being neglected by the vocational schools. Both types of complaints suggest that greater diversification of training programs is needed. The vocational school system would undoubtedly profit by a closer and more cooperative relationship among employers, labor unions, and school authorities in planning the programs to be offered and the number of youth to be admitted to those programs.

Still another reason which might be cited for the failure of many youth to find the sorts of work for which they had been trained was that the schools and public placement services helped a comparatively small minority of them to get jobs. Adequate guidance and training of youth are not enough by themselves. Efficient placement services operated in close collaboration with the vocational schools are necessary in order to prevent the skills acquired by trained youth from being lost through disuse. A weak link anywhere in this chain of three principal vocational services seriously impairs the effectiveness of the other two.

There is a definite need for expansion of the junior placement agencies and for their closer cooperation with the vocational schools. Efficient placement services could not only help youth to find the sorts of jobs they desire, but also help the vocational schools in each locality to gauge labor-market needs in various occupations.

All of these factors—lack of guidance, the unspecialized nature of some of the training programs, failure to coordinate training with labor-market needs in certain fields, and inadequate placement services—undoubtedly contributed to lowering the proportion of youth who found jobs related to their training. Probably more important than any single one of these, however, was a factor that was out of the control of vocational educators: the difficulty faced by youth in finding jobs during a period of depression. Not only were many trained youth completely unemployed during the depression, but many others took whatever jobs they could find regardless of their training. Once started in a new line of work, they tended to stay there, and many of them lost such skills as they had acquired in vocational school.

With the expansion of industrial production which started in 1939, more youth may be expected to graduate from vocational schools into jobs appropriate to their training. This fact has caused many persons to advocate the expansion of the vocational schools. Any large-scale expansion of training, however, should be based on a care-

ful analysis of labor-market needs, in order that the number of trainees will not far outrun the number of jobs available. Otherwise over-
keen competition for skilled jobs may undermine standards of wages
and working conditions which have been built up over many years;
and many youth may have their training wasted and their morale
lowered by failure to find jobs which they had been led to expect
would be waiting for them.

THE LARGER PROBLEM OF UNEMPLOYMENT

Vocational education is, of course, no cure for unemployment. It
cannot put youth in jobs where no jobs exist. It can help some youth
to make a more effective and less painful adjustment to the labor
market by training them efficiently in fields where jobs do exist. And
it may relieve the pressure on the labor market to some extent by (1)
keeping youth in school who would otherwise be working or seeking
work, and (2) helping to prevent bottlenecks in production which may
occasionally arise from shortages of skilled labor. The contraction
of the labor force, not only through the establishment of a higher level
of compulsory school attendance but also through the extension of
old-age retirement and pension legislation, would certainly tend to
result in decreased unemployment. Increased employment among
youth, however, must depend primarily upon the expansion of employment generally.

Eventually unemployment among youth may become less extensive
because of the expected drop in the proportion of young people in our
population and the decline in competition for jobs which may result.
But the problem cannot wait upon such a long-term solution. Youth
must have jobs here and now if their morale and skills are to be pre-
served. This is why the work programs—NYA, CCC, and WPA—
have been of great value to youth. In them young people not only
earn modest sums, but also learn and practice new skills, and acquire
the work experience they so badly need if they are to obtain private
employment. Public projects for youth should therefore be continued
and expanded as long as there are unemployed youth desirous of
obtaining such work in the United States. Every youth who leaves
school and cannot get a job should be provided with an opportunity
to do useful work under public auspices.[2] It is important to develop
and utilize the Nation's human resources in time of peace just as it is
in time of war; and it is almost as essential to maintain employment
and morale in consumers' goods industries as in war industries.

[2] In this connection, see the American Youth Commission bulletin, *Youth—
Their Jobs, Their Health, Their Schooling; A Program for Action*, Washington,
D. C., 1939.

The federally sponsored system of vocational training has come to be accepted as having two related functions in our industrial economy: the preparation of youth for useful work, and the supplying of trained workers for the needs of industry. To a considerable extent it has fulfilled these functions. With further study and improvement, vocational training can be of even greater value in the future than it has been in the past, both to youth and to the Nation.

Appendixes

Appendix A

TABLES

Table 1.—Enrollment in Vocational Schools in the United States Operated Under State (Smith-Hughes) Plans, by Year and Type of Program, 1918–1939

School year ending—	Total enroll- ment	Type of program			
		Agricultural	Trade and industrial	Home economics	Business education
1918	164, 123	15, 450	117, 934	30, 799	—
1919	194, 895	19, 933	135, 548	39, 414	—
1920	265, 058	31, 301	184, 819	48, 938	—
1921	324, 247	43, 352	217, 500	63, 395	—
1922	475, 828	60, 236	296, 884	118, 708	—
1923	536, 528	71, 298	325, 889	139, 341	—
1924	690, 055	89, 640	428, 473	171, 942	—
1925	792, 424	94, 765	490, 791	206, 868	—
1926	885, 275	111, 585	537, 738	235, 952	—
1927	911, 626	129, 032	564, 188	218, 406	—
1928	999, 031	147, 481	619, 548	232, 002	—
1929	1, 047, 976	171, 466	627, 397	249, 113	—
1930	1, 064, 536	193, 325	633, 153	238, 058	—
1931	1, 117, 556	237, 200	602, 755	227, 601	—
1932	1, 176, 162	257, 255	579, 591	339, 316	—
1933	1, 150, 327	265, 978	537, 512	346, 837	—
1934	1, 119, 140	289, 361	486, 058	343. 721	—
1935	1, 247, 523	329, 367	536, 932	381, 224	—
1936	1, 381, 701	347, 728	579, 971	454, 002	—
1937	1, 496, 837	394, 400	606, 212	496. 225	—
1938	1, 810, 082	460, 876	685, 804	627, 394	36, 008
1939 [1]	2, 085, 427	538, 586	715, 239	741, 503	90, 099

[1] Figures subject to revision.

Source: *Digest of Annual Reports of State Boards for Vocational Education to the U. S. Office of Education, Vocational Division, Fiscal Year Ended June 30, 1939*, U. S. Office of Education, Federal Security Agency, Washington, D. C., 1940, p. 3.

Table 2.—Enrollment in Vocational Schools or Classes in the United States Operated Under State (Smith-Hughes) Plans, by Type of School and Type of Program, Year Ended June 30, 1939 [1]

Type of school	Total enroll-ment	Type of program			
		Agricultural	Trade and industrial	Home economics	Business education
All types_____	2, 085, 427	538, 586	715, 239	741, 503	90, 099
Evening_____	657, 603	181, 962	156, 464	236, 034	83, 143
Part-time_____	486, 551	51, 593	362, 410	65, 592	6, 956
All-day_____	941, 273	305, 031	196, 365	439, 877	—
		Increase or decrease over 1938			
All types_____	275, 345	77, 710	29, 435	114, 109	54, 091
Evening_____	87, 895	23, 149	−6, 855	20, 866	50, 735
Part-time_____	47, 558	8, 693	24, 128	11, 381	3, 356
All-day_____	139, 892	45, 868	12, 162	81, 862	—

[1] Figures subject to revision.

Source: *Digest of Annual Reports of State Boards for Vocational Education to the U. S. Office of Education, Vocational Division, Fiscal Year Ended June 30, 1939*, U. S. Office of Education, Federal Security Agency, Washington, D. C., 1940, p. 2.

Table 3.—Percent Distribution of Vocationally Trained Youth and Other Youth, by Usual Occupation of Father and by City

Occupation of father	St. Louis	Birmingham	Denver	Seattle
Total vocationally trained youth [1]_____	2, 128	189	68	257
	Percent distribution			
Total_____	100	100	100	100
Professional_____	3	2	7	5
Proprietors, managers, and officials_____	16	23	10	16
Clerical_____	18	17	9	16
Skilled_____	30	42	33	33
Semiskilled_____	20	13	25	16
Unskilled_____	13	3	16	14
Total other youth [2]_____	4, 950	3, 087	3, 532	4, 187
	Percent distribution			
Total_____	100	100	100	100
Professional_____	4	5	6	8
Proprietors, managers, and officials_____	18	19	24	23
Clerical_____	16	16	18	17
Skilled_____	27	30	25	28
Semiskilled_____	23	13	15	13
Unskilled_____	12	17	12	11

[1] Excludes 400 youth whose fathers were deceased, absent, or with usual occupations which were not ascertainable. Based on 100-percent sample.
[2] Excludes 2,217 youth whose fathers were deceased, absent, or with usual occupations which were not ascertainable. Based on partial sample.

Table 4.—Percent Distribution of Vocationally Trained Youth and Other Youth, by Rental Value of Residence and by City

Rental value of residence	St. Louis	Birmingham	Denver	Seattle
Total vocationally trained youth_____	2,461	217	[1] 70	293
	Percent distribution			
Total_____	100	100	100	100
Low rental_____	19	13	57	29
Medium rental_____	56	52	40	56
High rental_____	25	35	3	15
Total other youth_____	5,583	3,686	4,006	4,698
	Percent distribution			
Total_____	100	100	100	100
Low rental_____	26	25	25	25
Medium rental_____	50	49	54	51
High rental_____	24	26	21	24

[1] Excludes 1 youth whose place of residence in terms of rental value was not ascertainable.

NOTE.—Data for vocationally trained youth are based on 100-percent sample; data for other youth are based on partial sample.

Table 5.—Percent Distribution of Vocationally Trained Youth and Other Youth, by Age at Eighth-Grade Graduation and by City

Age [1] at eighth-grade graduation	St. Louis	Birmingham	Denver	Seattle
Total vocationally trained youth_____	2,461	217	71	293
	Percent distribution			
Total_____	100	100	100	100
12 years and under_____	9	6	6	3
13 years_____	34	18	30	33
14 years_____	36	38	33	42
15 years_____	16	18	24	18
16 years and over_____	5	20	7	4
Total other youth_____	5,583	3,686	4,006	4,698
	Percent distribution			
Total_____	100	100	100	100
12 years and under_____	7	12	3	4
13 years_____	32	32	35	30
14 years_____	37	30	43	42
15 years_____	17	16	15	18
16 years and over_____	7	10	4	6
Median age, vocationally trained youth__	14.2	14.7	14.4	14.3
Median age, other youth_____	14.3	14.2	14.3	14.4

[1] Age at last birthday.

NOTE.—Data for vocationally trained youth are based on 100-percent sample; data for other youth are based on partial sample.

450596°– 42——

Table 6.—Year of Eighth-Grade Graduation of Vocationally Trained Youth, by City

Year of eighth-grade graduation	Total 4 cities	St. Louis	Birmingham	Denver	Seattle
Total vocationally trained youth	3,042	2,461	217	71	293
1929	953	781	84	24	64
1931	1,187	1,012	61	27	87
1933	902	668	72	20	142

Table 7.—Percent Distribution of Vocationally Trained Youth, by Years of Education Completed and by City

Years of education completed	Total 4 cities	St. Louis	Birmingham	Denver	Seattle
Total vocationally trained youth	3,042	2,461	217	71	293
	Percent distribution				
Total	100	100	100	100	100
8 years	3	3	—	6	1
9 years	12	13	8	13	3
10 years	18	20	20	11	7
11 years	20	20	37	18	8
12 years	44	41	33	46	77
13 years	1	1	1	3	2
14 years	1	1	1	—	2
15 years	*	*	*	—	*
16 years	1	1	*	3	—
17 years and over	—	—	—	—	—
Median	11.9	11.7	11.6	12.0	12.4

* Less than 0.5 percent.

Table 8.—Sex Distribution of Vocationally Trained Youth, by City

Sex	Total 4 cities	St. Louis	Birmingham	Denver	Seattle
Total vocationally trained youth	3,042	2,461	217	71	293
Male	1,308	984	152	71	101
Female	1,734	1,477	65	—	192
	Percent distribution				
Total	100	100	100	100	100
Male	43	40	70	100	34
Female	57	60	30	—	66

Table 9.—Percent Distribution of Vocationally Trained Youth, by Age at Time of Interview and by City

Age at time of interview	Total 4 cities	St. Louis	Birmingham	Denver	Seattle
Total vocationally trained youth	3,042	2,461	217	71	293
	Percent distribution				
Total	100	100	100	100	100
17 years and under	1	1	1	—	1
18 years	7	7	1	3	13
19 years	14	13	12	15	22
20 years	17	17	12	23	16
21 years	20	21	21	15	18
22 years	18	18	18	21	10
23 years	15	15	17	6	13
24 years	6	6	12	10	6
25 years and over	2	2	6	7	1
Median	21.6	21.6	22.2	21.6	20.9

Table 10.—Youth Enrolled in Smith-Hughes Training Programs, by Program and City

Training program	Total 4 cities	St. Louis	Birmingham	Denver	Seattle
All programs	[1] 3,034	2,456	216	69	293
Commercial programs	1,549	1,425	39	—	85
Accounting	40	40	—	—	—
Bookkeeping	29	26	—	—	3
Calculating machines	2	1	—	—	1
Clerical	52	52	—	—	—
Distributive programs	59	24	[2] 35	—	—
General business	225	144	—	—	[3] 81
General commercial	283	279	[4] 4	—	—
Secretarial	301	301	—	—	—
Special commercial	315	315	—	—	—
Stenography	243	243	—	—	—
Industrial programs	986	703	137	69	77
Aeromechanics	39	39	—	—	—
Auto mechanics	191	115	19	36	21
Boatbuilding	6	—	—	—	6
Drafting	68	56	12	—	—
Electricity	193	147	15	16	15
General industrial	20	10	—	—	10
Horticulture	1	1	—	—	—
Machine shop	164	112	24	17	11
Painting and decorating	25	8	17	—	—
Printing	106	80	20	—	6
Radio	31	3	20	—	8
Sheet metal	57	57	—	—	—
Woodworking	85	75	10	—	—
Women's programs	385	232	29	—	124
Cafeteria-tearoom	61	48	13	—	—
Clothing	17	—	2	—	[5] 15
Cosmetology	92	50	[6] 3	—	[6] 39
Dry cleaning	12	—	—	—	12
Industrial sewing	136	111	—	—	[7] 25
Home economics	44	23	11	—	[8] 10
Millinery	3	—	—	—	3
Tailoring	20	—	—	—	20
Arts programs	114	96	11	—	7
Arts and crafts	4	4	—	—	—
Commercial art	75	57	11	—	7
Show-card writing	35	35	—	—	—

[1] Excludes 8 youth whose training programs were not ascertainable (5 in St. Louis, 1 in Birmingham, and 2 in Denver).
[2] Retailing. See table 11.
[3] Business training (normally on a part-time basis, but because of the advanced nature of the work, considered full-time training for the purposes of this survey).
[4] Office practice.
[5] Commercial dressmaking.
[6] Beauty culture.
[7] Power sewing.
[8] Home service.

Table 11.—Sex and Completion of Training of Labor-Market Entrants, by Selected Training Program and by City

City and program	Total labor-market entrants	Males		Females		Males with completed training		Females with completed training	
		Number	Percent	Number	Percent	Number	Percent of all males	Number	Percent of all females
4 cities	2,857	1,263	44	1,594	56	401	32	680	43
St. Louis	¹ 2,354	961	41	1,393	59	268	28	561	40
Commercial programs	1,348	205	15	1,143	85	90	44	452	40
General commercial	264	22	8	242	92	2	9	36	15
General business	141	24	17	117	83	7	29	33	28
Stenography	237	11	5	226	95	3	†	87	38
Accounting	37	33	89	4	11	18	55	2	†
Clerical	51	8	16	43	84	2	†	3	7
Secretarial	280	57	20	223	80	36	63	157	70
Special commercial	290	41	14	249	86	20	49	118	47
Industrial programs	699	698	100	1	*	169	24	—	—
Aeromechanics	39	39	100	—	—	15	38	—	—
Drafting	56	56	100	—	—	22	39	—	—
Auto mechanics	114	114	100	—	—	30	26	—	—
Electricity	145	145	100	—	—	40	28	—	—
Machine shop	112	112	100	—	—	33	29	—	—
Printing	80	79	99	1	1	20	25	—	—
Sheet metal	57	57	100	—	—	3	5	—	—
Woodworking	74	74	100	—	—	2	3	—	—
Women's programs	216	1	*	215	100	—	—	87	40
Cafeteria-tearoom	46	—	—	46	100	—	—	11	24
Cosmetology	47	—	—	47	100	—	—	45	96
Industrial sewing	103	—	—	103	100	—	—	31	30
Arts programs	91	57	63	34	37	9	16	22	65
Commercial art	54	24	44	30	56	8	33	20	67
Show-card writing	33	29	88	4	12	1	3	2	†
Birmingham	204	149	73	55	27	77	52	21	38
Retailing	31	9	29	22	71	6	†	7	32
Denver	68	68	100	—	—	20	29	—	—
Auto mechanics	36	36	100	—	—	7	19	—	—
Seattle	231	85	37	146	63	36	42	98	67
Beauty culture	31	—	—	31	100	—	—	28	90
Business training	59	7	12	52	88	2	†	29	56

*Less than 0.5 percent.
†Percent not figured on base of less than 20 persons.
¹ Excludes 4 St. Louis youth whose status with regard to completion was not ascertainable.
NOTE.—Programs with fewer than 25 labor-market entrants are excluded, except from totals and subtotals.

Table 12.—Youth Completing Selected Vocational Training Programs, by City

City and program	Total youth enrolled	Youth completing training	
		Number	Percent
4 cities	[1] 3,034	1,131	37
St. Louis	2,456	867	35
Commercial programs	1,425	573	40
General commercial	279	40	14
General business	144	41	28
Stenography	243	91	37
Accounting	40	21	53
Bookkeeping and billing machines	26	8	31
Clerical	52	5	10
Secretarial	301	208	69
Special commercial	315	148	47
Industrial programs	703	170	24
Aeromechanics	39	15	38
Drafting	56	22	39
Auto mechanics	115	30	26
Electricity	147	41	28
Machine shop	112	33	29
Printing	80	20	25
Sheet metal	57	3	5
Woodworking	75	2	3
Women's programs	232	92	40
Cafeteria-tearoom	48	12	25
Cosmetology	50	47	94
Industrial sewing	111	33	30
Arts programs	96	32	33
Commercial art	57	28	49
Show-card writing	35	4	11
Birmingham	216	103	48
Retailing	35	13	37
Denver	69	20	29
Auto mechanics	36	7	19
Seattle	293	141	48
Beauty culture	39	29	74
Power sewing	25	18	72
Business training	81	34	42

[1] Excludes 8 youth, the status of completion of whose training was not ascertainable.

NOTE.—Programs with fewer than 25 registrants among the youth studied are excluded, except from the totals and subtotals.

Table 13.—Percent Distribution of Youth With Incomplete Vocational Training, by Reason for Failure To Complete Training, by City, Sex, and Year of Eighth-Grade Graduation

Reason for failure to complete training	Total youth with incomplete training	City				Sex		Eighth-grade class		
		St. Louis	Bir-ming-ham	Den-ver	Seat-tle	Male	Fe-male	1929	1931	1933
Total youth_____	[1] 1,839	1,584	113	51	91	869	970	593	715	531
	Percent distribution									
Total youth_____	100	100	100	100	100	100	100	100	100	100
Preference for work_____	32	34	23	16	32	40	27	32	32	33
Lack of funds_____	28	29	25	27	21	30	27	27	30	28
Lack of interest_____	22	22	18	25	13	17	26	24	21	20
Preference for other type of education_____	6	5	15	6	9	6	5	4	7	6
Physical disability_____	2	2	—	4	6	1	3	2	2	4
Marriage_____	1	*	7	—	4	*	1	—	*	1
Other_____	9	8	12	22	15	6	11	11	8	8

*Less than 0.5 percent.

[1] Excludes 72 youth, status of completion of whose training was not ascertainable.

Table 14.—Percent Distribution of Vocationally Trained Youth, by City, Selected Program, and Usual Occupation of Father

City and program	Total youth	Percent distribution by usual occupation of father					
		Total	Professional	Proprietors, managers, and officials	Clerical	Skilled	Semi-skilled	Unskilled
4 cities	1 2,634	100	2	16	18	31	20	13
St. Louis	2,123	100	3	16	18	30	20	13
Commercial programs	1,224	100	4	17	21	29	19	10
General commercial	222	100	2	12	12	31	21	22
General business	121	100	2	13	17	31	25	12
Stenography	201	100	4	18	17	32	20	9
Accounting	38	100	8	24	34	23	8	3
Clerical	46	100	2	15	20	26	28	9
Secretarial	273	100	7	18	32	27	12	4
Special commercial	279	100	3	19	24	27	18	9
Industrial programs	617	100	2	16	14	29	26	13
Aeromechanics	34	100	6	12	12	35	29	6
Drafting	48	100	2	10	27	23	21	17
Auto mechanics	96	100	1	19	15	32	20	13
Electricity	129	100	2	8	19	29	29	13
Machine shop	97	100	2	19	7	23	37	12
Printing	74	100	—	22	13	32	23	10
Sheet metal	50	100	2	18	10	24	24	22
Woodworking	68	100	—	16	15	35	19	15
Women's programs	197	100	3	11	9	25	18	34
Cafeteria-tearoom	42	100	5	14	14	26	22	19
Cosmetology	43	100	—	16	2	19	12	51
Industrial sewing	96	100	4	8	11	29	21	27
Arts programs	85	100	5	19	13	40	14	9
Commercial art	49	100	6	27	18	35	8	6
Show-card writing	33	100	3	9	6	49	18	15
Birmingham	188	100	2	23	18	41	13	3
Retailing	29	100	—	10	28	48	10	4
Denver	66	100	8	11	8	31	25	17
Auto mechanics	34	100	9	6	9	35	26	·15
Seattle	257	100	5	16	16	33	16	14
Beauty culture	34	100	12	12	20	29	15	12
Business training	75	100	5	24	20	23	13	15

1 Excludes 408 youth whose fathers were deceased, absent, or with usual occupations which were not ascertainable.

NOTE.—Programs with fewer than 25 registrants whose fathers' occupations were ascertainable are excluded except from totals and subtotals.

Table 15.—Activity Status on July 1, 1938, of all Youth Interviewed, by Type of Vocational Training and by City [1]

City and type of vocational training	Total Youth	Percent distribution br activity status				
		Total	Entered labor market at some time	Status on July 1, 1938		
				In labor market	In school	Not seeking work
4 cities	19, 116	100	85	69	12	19
Smith-Hughes training	1, 139	100	94	81	6	13
No Smith-Hughes training	17, 977	100	85	67	13	20
Regular high-school vocational training (Seattle only)	1, 326	100	89	71	11	18
Private school vocational training	1, 768	100	92	74	9	17
No vocational training	14, 883	100	83	67	13	20
St. Louis	6, 429	100	91	77	7	16
Smith-Hughes training	846	100	95	83	4	13
No Smith-Hughes training	5, 583	100	91	77	7	16
Private school vocational training	808	100	94	80	7	13
No vocational training	4, 775	100	90	76	8	16
Birmingham	3, 827	100	85	65	10	25
Smith-Hughes training	138	100	96	84	3	13
No Smith-Hughes training	3, 689	100	84	64	11	25
Private school vocational training	225	100	95	75	6	19
No vocational training	3, 464	100	84	64	11	25
Denver	4, 019	100	82	64	15	21
Smith-Hughes training	13	100	†	†	—	†
No Smith-Hughes training	4, 006	100	82	64	15	21
Private school vocational training	487	100	90	66	11	23
No vocational training	3, 519	100	81	64	15	21
Seattle	4, 841	100	80	63	18	19
Smith-Hughes training	142	100	80	66	23	11
No Smith-Hughes training	4, 699	100	80	63	18	19
Regular high-school vocational training	1, 326	100	89	71	11	18
Private school vocational training	248	100	86	67	15	18
No vocational training	3, 125	100	76	59	22	19

† Percent not computed on base of less than 25.

[1] Based on the partial sample of all youth in the 4 cities, excluding additional sample of vocationally trained youth.

Table 16.—Labor-Market Status of Trained Youth Who Graduated from the Eighth Grade in 1929, by Month and by Sex, January 1929–July 1938

[4 cities]

Year and month ¹	Labor-market status of trained youth who graduated from the eighth grade in 1929										
	Male ²					Female ³					
	Total	In school	Others not seeking work	Employed	Unemployed	Total	In school	Housewives	Others not seeking work	Employed	Unemployed
1929											
January	100	100	—	—	—	100	100	—	—	—	—
February	100	99	—	1	—	100	99	—	*	*	*
March	100	99	—	1	—	100	99	—	*	*	1
April	100	99	—	1	—	100	99	—	*	*	1
May	100	99	—	1	—	100	99	—	*	*	*
June	100	99	—	1	*	100	99	—	*	*	1
July	100	96	*	3	1	100	97	—	1	1	1
August	100	96	*	3	1	100	97	—	1	1	1
September	100	96	*	3	1	100	97	—	1	1	1
October	100	97	*	3	—	100	97	—	1	1	1
November	100	96	*	4	—	100	97	—	1	1	1
December	100	96	*	4	—	100	98	—	1	1	*
1930											
January	100	96	*	4	—	100	97	—	2	1	*
February	100	96	—	4	—	100	97	—	1	1	1
March	100	95	—	5	—	100	97	—	1	1	1
April	100	94	—	5	1	100	96	—	1	2	1
May	100	93	—	6	1	100	96	—	1	2	1
June	100	93	—	6	1	100	96	—	1	2	1
July	100	90	—	9	1	100	91	—	3	4	2
August	100	90	—	9	1	100	92	—	2	4	2
September	100	90	—	9	1	100	91	—	2	4	3
October	100	90	—	9	1	100	93	—	1	4	2
November	100	90	—	9	1	100	92	—	1	5.	2
December	100	89	—	10	1	100	92	—	1	5	2
1931											
January	100	90	—	9	1	100	92	*	1	4	3
February	100	88	—	11	1	100	89	*	3	5	3
March	100	87	—	12	1	100	88	*	3	6	3
April	100	87	—	12	1	100	88	*	3	6	3
May	100	86	—	13	1	100	86	*	3	7	4
June	100	83	1	14	2	100	85	*	4	7	4
July	100	78	2	16	4	100	77	*	7	10	6
August	100	78	2	16	4	100	77	*	7	10	6
September	100	79	2	16	3	100	78	*	6	10	6
October	100	79	2	16	3	100	78	*	4	12	6
November	100	79	2	16	3	100	78	*	4	12	6
December	100	78	2	17	3	100	78	*	5	12	5
1932											
January	100	77	3	16	4	100	77	1	4	12	6
February	100	75	3	17	5	100	74	1	5	14	6
March	100	76	3	17	4	100	73	1	6	15	5
April	100	76	2	18	4	100	74	1	5	15	5
May	100	75	2	19	4	100	72	1	5	16	6
June	100	73	3	19	5	100	71	1	6	15	7
July	100	66	3	24	7	100	62	1	7	18	12
August	100	66	3	24	7	100	62	2	7	18	11
September	100	66	3	24	7	100	61	2	7	19	11
October	100	66	3	24	7	100	62	2	6	20	10
November	100	66	4	24	6	100	61	2	6	22	9
December	100	64	3	27	6	100	61	2	6	22	9
1933											
January	100	64	3	26	7	100	60	2	6	23	9
February	100	57	3	31	9	100	56	2	7	25	10
March	100	57	3	33	7	100	55	2	7	26	10
April	100	56	3	34	7	100	54	3	6	28	9
May	100	56	3	34	7	100	53	3	6	28	10
June	100	54	4	34	8	100	52	3	7	28	10
July	100	38	6	43	13	100	37	3	10	31	19
August	100	39	5	44	12	100	36	3	10	33	18
September	100	38	6	44	12	100	37	3	10	34	16
October	100	40	6	41	13	100	37	3	8	36	16
November	100	40	6	40	14	100	36	4	8	37	15
December	100	40	5	42	13	100	36	4	7	37	16

See footnotes at end of table.

Table 16.—Labor-Market Status of Trained Youth Who Graduated from the Eighth Grade in 1929, by Month and by Sex, January 1929–July 1938—Continued

[4 cities]

Year and month [1]	Labor-market status of trained youth who graduated from the eighth grade in 1929										
	Male [2]					Female [3]					
	Total	In school	Others not seeking work	Employed	Unemployed	Total	In school	Housewives	Others not seeking work	Employed	Unemployed
1934											
January	100	39	5	43	13	100	36	4	7	38	15
February	100	31	5	48	16	100	33	5	8	38	16
March	100	31	5	50	14	100	32	5	8	39	16
April	100	30	5	51	14	100	32	6	8	39	15
May	100	29	4	53	14	100	31	6	8	41	14
June	100	27	4	56	13	100	29	6	7	43	15
July	100	15	6	60	19	100	16	7	8	48	21
August	100	15	5	62	18	100	16	7	8	48	21
September	100	15	5	63	17	100	16	7	8	50	19
October	100	19	4	63	14	100	19	7	6	51	17
November	100	18	4	63	15	100	18	7	6	53	16
December	100	18	4	63	15	100	18	7	6	54	15
1935											
January	100	18	3	63	16	100	18	8	5	54	15
February	100	15	4	63	18	100	16	8	5	56	15
March	100	15	3	65	17	100	16	8	5	56	15
April	100	14	3	66	17	100	14	9	5	58	14
May	100	13	3	68	16	100	14	9	5	58	14
June	100	12	3	70	15	100	12	9	5	59	15
July	100	6	2	74	18	100	7	9	6	62	16
August	100	6	2	76	16	100	6	9	6	63	16
September	100	6	2	77	15	100	6	10	6	62	16
October	100	7	1	78	14	100	7	10	6	63	14
November	100	7	1	77	15	100	7	11	5	64	13
December	100	7	1	77	15	100	7	11	4	65	13
1936											
January	100	6	2	77	15	100	7	11	4	66	12
February	100	6	2	78	14	100	6	12	4	66	12
March	100	6	2	79	13	100	6	12	4	66	12
April	100	6	2	81	11	100	5	13	4	67	11
May	100	5	2	83	10	100	6	13	4	67	10
June	100	5	2	83	10	100	5	14	4	67	10
July	100	4	1	86	9	100	4	14	4	68	10
August	100	4	2	86	8	100	3	14	4	69	10
September	100	4	2	85	9	100	3	14	4	70	9
October	100	5	1	85	9	100	4	15	4	69	8
November	100	5	1	86	8	100	4	15	3	71	7
December	100	5	1	86	8	100	4	15	3	71	7
1937											
January	100	4	1	86	9	100	4	16	3	71	6
February	100	5	1	85	9	100	3	16	3	72	6
March	100	4	1	87	8	100	3	17	3	71	6
April	100	3	1	89	7	100	3	18	3	70	6
May	100	3	1	89	7	100	3	18	3	69	7
June	100	3	1	91	5	100	2	18	3	70	7
July	100	2	1	90	7	100	2	19	4	69	6
August	100	2	1	90	7	100	2	19	4	69	6
September	100	2	1	89	8	100	2	19	4	68	7
October	100	3	1	89	7	100	2	19	4	69	6
November	100	3	1	89	7	100	2	19	4	69	6
December	100	3	1	88	8	100	2	20	4	68	6
1938											
January	100	4	1	85	10	100	2	20	3	69	6
February	100	4	1	83	12	100	2	20	3	68	7
March	100	4	1	85	10	100	2	20	3	68	7
April	100	4	1	84	11	100	1	21	4	67	7
May	100	4	1	85	10	100	1	21	3	67	8
June	100	4	1	84	11	100	1	22	3	66	8
July	100	1	1	85	13	100	1	22	3	66	

* Less than 0.5 percent.

[1] Data as of first of each month.
[2] Base throughout period studied was 357.
[3] Base throughout period studied was 567.

Table 17.—Employment Status of Youth in the Labor Market on July 1, 1938, by Sex, Type of Vocational Training, and City [1]

Sex and type of vocational training	St. Louis	Birmingham	Denver	Seattle
Total youth in labor market_____	4,980	2,487	2,587	3,044
	Percent employed, July 1, 1938			
Total_____	81	72	84	82
Smith-Hughes training_____	83	76	88	78
No Smith-Hughes training_____	81	72	84	82
Regular high-school vocational training (Seattle only)_____	—	—	—	83
Private school vocational training_____	86	85	89	88
No vocational training_____	80	71	83	82
Male_____	81	74	85	83
Smith-Hughes training_____	83	78	88	81
No Smith-Hughes training_____	81	74	85	83
Regular high-school vocational training____	—	—	—	82
Private school vocational training_____	89	86	87	86
No vocational training_____	80	74	85	83
Female_____	81	70	83	81
Smith-Hughes training_____	82	68	—	75
No Smith-Hughes training_____	81	70	89	78
Regular high-school vocational training____	—	—	—	84
Private school vocational training_____	85	85	89	89
No vocational training_____	80	68	81	78

[1] Based on the partial sample of all youth in the 4 cities, except for the Smith-Hughes group, percentages for which are based on the expanded 100-percent sample of vocationally trained youth.

Table 18.—Employment Status of Trained Youth in the Labor Market on July 1, 1938, by Completion of Training and by City, 4 Cities, and by Race in St. Louis

City and completion of training	Total trained youth in labor market		Employment status, July 1, 1938					
			Employed			Unemployed		
	Number	Percent	Total	Full time (30 hours or more per week)	Part time (under 30 hours per week)	Total	Seeking work or on layoff	Work programs
St. Louis_____	2,064	100	83	76	7	17	15	2
Smith-Hughes complete_____	759	100	82	76	6	18	17	1
Smith-Hughes incomplete_____	1,305	100	83	76	7	17	14	3
Birmingham_____	175	100	76	73	3	24	22	2
Smith-Hughes complete_____	83	100	80	76	4	20	19	1
Smith-Hughes incomplete_____	92	100	73	70	3	27	24	3
Denver_____	68	100	88	78	10	12	6	6
Smith-Hughes complete_____	20	†	†	†	†	†	†	—
Smith-Hughes incomplete_____	48	100	85	73	12	15	6	9
Seattle_____	178	100	78	67	11	22	20	2
Smith-Hughes complete_____	113	100	80	73	7	20	20	—
Smith-Hughes incomplete_____	65	100	74	57	17	26	21	5
St. Louis: White_____	1,972	100	84	78	6	16	15	1
Negro_____	92	100	60	36	24	40	23	17

† Percent not computed on base of less than 25.

Table 19.—Average Weekly Earnings on all Full-Time Jobs of Smith-Hughes Youth, by Completion of Training and by City

| City | Average weekly earnings on all full-time jobs | | |
	Total trained youth	Youth with completed training	Youth with incomplete training
St. Louis	$14.70	$14.60	$14.70
Birmingham	15.40	16.00	15.00
Denver [1]	15.30	15.40	15.20
Seattle	15.10	15.00	15.30

[1] Males only.

Table 20.—Average [1] Time in the Labor Market and Time Employed, Smith-Hughes Trained Youth and other Youth, by City

| City | Smith-Hughes trained youth | | | Other youth | | |
	Average [1] months in labor market	Average [1] months employed	Percent of labor-market time employed [2]	Average [1] months in labor market	Average [1] months employed	Percent of labor-market time employed [2]
St. Louis	42	33	79	49	39	80
Completed training	32	25	79	—	—	—
Incomplete training	47	37	79	—	—	—
Birmingham	37	31	84	33	25	76
Denver	47	40	87	36	31	86
Seattle	25	21	83	32	26	81

[1] Mean.
[2] Computed from averages figured to 1 decimal point.

Table 21.—Percent Distribution of Smith-Hughes Trained Youth and Other Youth, by Weekly Earnings on Full-Time Jobs, June 1, 1938, and by City [1]

Weekly earnings [2] on full-time jobs, June 1, 1938	St. Louis		Birmingham		Denver		Seattle	
	Smith-Hughes trained youth	Other youth	Smith-Hughes trained youth	Other youth	Smith-Hughes trained youth [4]	Other youth	Smith-Hughes trained youth	Other youth
Total youth___	1,541	3,147	127	1,446	52	1,987	115	2,044
	Percent distribution							
Total_____	100	100	100	100	100	100	100	100
$1–$5_____	1	1	1	6	—	1	2	1
$6–$9_____	3	3	2	13	6	4	6	3
$10_____	4	5	6	6	4	5	3	2
$11–$12_____	9	9	5	8	10	7	4	4
$13–$14_____	14	15	12	11	2	14	5	6
$15_____	16	13	9	8	13	13	11	9
$16–$17_____	17	13	9	9	6	11	16	12
$18–$19_____	11	12	18	9	13	13	12	11
$20_____	8	8	10	8	10	9	12	9
$21–$24_____	7	8	11	9	11	9	13	13
$25–$29_____	6	7	8	7	19	9	8	14
$30–$34_____	2	3	6	3	2	3	3	8
$35–$39_____	1	2	1	1	4	1	3	4
$40–$49_____	1	1	2	1	—	1	2	3
$50–$59_____	*	*	—	*	—	*	—	*
$60 and more_____	*	*	—	*	—	*	—	1
Average [3]_____	$16.00	$16.10	$18.20	$15.20	$18.90	$16.80	$17.90	$19.60

*Less than 0.5 percent.

[1] Figures for "Other youth" are based on regular sample only. Figures for Smith-Hughes trained youth are based on the expanded sample. Youth not working on full-time jobs on July 1, 1938, are excluded.
[2] Rounded to the nearest dollar.
[3] Based on more detailed distribution than that given in table.
[4] Males only.

Table 22.—Occupations of Vocationally Trained Youth on First Full-Time Jobs and of Vocationally Trained Youth and All Youth on Full-Time Jobs on July 1, 1938, by City

City and occupation of youth	Percent distribution		
	Smith-Hughes trained youth only		All youth [1]
	First full-time jobs	Full-time jobs held on July 1, 1938	Full-time jobs held on July 1, 1938
St. Louis	100	100	100
Professional	2	3	2
Proprietors, managers, and officials	1	1	2
Clerical	51	54	50
Skilled	4	7	4
Semiskilled	33	29	34
Unskilled	9	6	8
Birmingham	100	100	100
Professional	2	2	3
Proprietors, managers, and officials	3	3	4
Clerical	37	36	45
Skilled	11	17	5
Semiskilled	31	38	23
Unskilled	16	4	20
Denver	100	100	100
Professional	5	10	2
Proprietors, managers, and officials	—	—	5
Clerical	29	17	37
Skilled	8	14	8
Semiskilled	36	46	35
Unskilled	22	13	13
Seattle	100	100	100
Professional	1	2	2
Proprietors, managers, and officials	1	4	3
Clerical	27	28	47
Skilled	3	5	4
Semiskilled	42	49	28
Unskilled	26	12	16

[1] Male youth only were included in the Denver figures for "all youth" to make them comparable to the figures for trained youth.

Table 23.—Occupations of Smith-Hughes Trained Youth on First Full-Time Jobs, by Selected Training Program and by City

City and program	Total youth with first full-time jobs		Professional	Proprietors, managers, and officials	Clerical	Skilled	Semiskilled	Unskilled
	Number	Percent						
4 cities	2,598	100	2	1	48	5	33	11
St. Louis	2,149	100	2	1	51	4	33	9
Commercial programs	1,211	100	*	1	72	1	20	6
General commercial	235	100	—	1	55	*	31	13
General business	122	100	—	—	64	1	26	9
Stenography	223	100	—	—	74	—	21	5
Accounting	36	100	—	8	73	8	8	3
Clerical	49	100	—	—	47	—	37	16
Secretarial	241	100	1	*	87	*	9	3
Special commercial	261	100	1	—	79	—	16	4
Industrial programs	667	100	2	1	26	12	48	11
Aeromechanics	36	100	3	—	25	11	50	11
Drafting	53	100	11	—	32	9	42	6
Auto mechanics	107	100	—	4	28	17	41	10
Electricity	135	100	1	—	24	9	53	13
Machine shop	109	100	1	—	16	15	60	8
Printing	78	100	3	—	22	20	46	9
Sheet metal	57	100	2	3	30	5	35	25
Woodworking	72	100	1	1	31	11	45	11
Women's programs	185	100	1	—	18	—	59	22
Cafeteria-tearoom	40	100	—	—	35	—	33	32
Cosmetology	40	100	2	—	5	—	83	10
Industrial sewing	93	100	1	—	19	—	65	15
Arts programs	86	100	27	—	35	6	24	8
Commercial art	49	100	43	—	33	2	16	6
Show-card writing	33	100	6	—	40	9	33	12
Birmingham	191	100	2	3	37	11	31	16
Retailing	27	100	—	—	70	—	11	19
Denver	63	100	5	—	29	8	36	22
Auto mechanics	34	100	9	—	27	6	32	26
Seattle	195	100	1	1	27	3	42	26
Beauty culture	29	100	—	—	14	—	72	14
Business training	40	100	—	—	70	—	12	18

* Less than 0.5 percent.

NOTE.—Programs with fewer than 25 youth who had held one job or more are excluded except from the totals and subtotals.

Table 24.—Occupations of Smith-Hughes Trained Youth on Full-Time Jobs Held on July 1, 1938, by Selected Training Program and by City

City and program	Total youth with full-time jobs on July 1, 1938		Professional	Proprietors, managers, and officials	Clerical	Skilled	Semi-skilled	Unskilled
	Number	Percent						
4 cities	1,863	100	3	2	50	7	32	6
St. Louis	1,565	100	3	1	54	7	29	6
Commercial programs	858	100	1	1	76	1	17	4
General commercial	136	100	—	—	57	1	32	10
General business	87	100	—	—	73	1	21	5
Stenography	159	100	—	—	81	1	14	4
Accounting	29	100	7	7	69	7	10	—
Clerical	30	100	—	—	43	—	40	17
Secretarial	203	100	1	1	88	1	7	2
Special commercial	186	100	1	—	84	1	13	1
Industrial programs	523	100	3	2	26	17	44	8
Aeromechanics	26	100	—	—	19	23	50	8
Drafting	44	100	18	5	27	16	29	5
Auto mechanics	79	100	1	4	28	18	40	9
Electricity	106	100	2	1	30	16	45	6
Machine shop	86	100	2	1	12	14	62	9
Printing	65	100	3	5	37	23	20	12
Sheet metal	46	100	—	2	26	13	48	11
Woodworking	54	100	2	—	30	11	51	6
Women's programs	114	100	2	—	23	—	66	9
Cosmetology	33	100	3	—	12	—	79	6
Industrial sewing	58	100	2	—	22	—	71	5
Arts programs	70	100	30	1	32	16	20	1
Commercial art	36	100	50	3	33	6	8	—
Show-card writing	28	100	11	—	35	25	25	4
Birmingham	127	100	2	3	36	17	38	4
Denver	52	100	—	10	17	14	46	13
Auto mechanics	25	100	—	20	12	24	36	8
Seattle	119	100	2	4	28	5	49	12

NOTE.—Programs with fewer than 25 youth who were working on July 1, 1938, are excluded except from the totals and subtotals.

Table 25.—Percent Distribution of Trained Labor-Market Entrants According to Relationship of Job to Training, by City, Sex, and Completion of Training

City, sex, and completion of training	Total labor-market entrants	Percent distribution of youth according to relationship of job to training					
		Total	With related jobs			No relationship	No jobs of 15 hours or more per week
			Total	Primary relationship	Secondary relationship only		
4 cities	2,857	100	59	46	13	33	8
Male	1,263	100	55	40	15	40	5
Complete	401	100	73	61	12	21	6
Incomplete	862	100	47	31	16	49	4
Female	1,594	100	62	51	11	27	11
Complete	680	100	74	63	11	14	12
Incomplete	914	100	52	42	10	38	10
St. Louis	2,354	100	59	47	12	33	8
Male	961	100	56	41	15	40	4
Complete	268	100	76	64	12	18	6
Incomplete	693	100	48	32	16	48	4
Female	1,393	100	62	51	11	28	10
Complete	561	100	74	62	12	14	12
Incomplete	832	100	54	44	10	38	8
Birmingham	204	100	58	41	17	37	5
Male	149	100	58	44	14	40	2
Complete	77	100	71	59	12	25	4
Incomplete	72	100	44	27	17	56	
Female	55	100	58	33	25	31	11
Complete	21	100	57	33	24	33	10
Incomplete	34	100	59	32	27	29	12
Denver (all male)	68	100	40	25	15	54	6
Complete	20	100	60	50	10	40	—
Incomplete	48	100	31	15	16	61	8
Seattle	231	100	62	55	7	20	18
Male	85	100	60	46	14	25	15
Complete	36	100	69	60	9	17	14
Incomplete	49	100	53	35	18	31	16
Female	146	100	63	60	3	17	20
Complete	98	100	81	77	4	8	11
Incomplete	48	100	27	25	2	35	38

Table 26.—Percent Distribution of Trained Labor-Market Entrants According to Relationship of Job to Training, by City and Selected Program

City and program	Total labor-market entrants	Percent distribution of youth according to relationship of job to training					
		Total	With related job			No relationship	No jobs of 15 hours or more per week
			Total	Primary relationship	Secondary relationship only		
4 cities	2,857	100	59	46	13	33	8
St. Louis	2,354	100	59	47	12	33	8
Commercial programs	1,348	100	63	50	13	28	9
General commercial	264	100	46	38	8	45	9
General business	141	100	54	50	4	34	12
Stenography	237	100	66	42	24	29	5
Accounting	37	100	78	51	27	22	—
Clerical	51	100	35	35	—	63	2
Secretarial	280	100	72	58	14	14	14
Special commercial	290	100	78	64	14	13	9
Industrial programs	699	100	54	40	14	42	4
Aeromechanics	39	100	61	28	33	36	3
Drafting	56	100	50	36	14	45	5
Auto mechanics	114	100	54	28	26	41	5
Electricity	145	100	57	48	9	38	5
Machine shop	112	100	75	63	12	23	2
Printing	80	100	59	58	1	39	2
Sheet metal	57	100	32	14	18	68	—
Woodworking	74	100	30	19	11	67	3
Women's programs	216	100	54	51	3	33	13
Cafeteria-tearoom	46	100	45	30	15	44	11
Cosmetology	47	100	83	83	—	6	11
Industrial sewing	103	100	46	46	—	44	10
Arts programs	91	100	52	38	14	46	2
Commercial art	54	100	59	50	9	37	4
Show-card writing	33	100	33	18	15	67	—
Birmingham	204	100	58	41	17	37	5
Commercial programs	34	100	70	32	38	18	12
Retailing	31	100	77	35	42	13	10
Industrial programs	136	100	57	44	13	41	2
Women's programs	26	100	54	35	19	38	8
Denver	68	100	40	25	15	54	6
Auto mechanics	36	100	47	25	22	47	6
Seattle	231	100	62	55	7	20	18
Commercial programs	63	100	54	51	3	14	32
Business training	59	100	54	52	2	12	34
Industrial programs	64	100	66	47	19	23	11
Women's programs	102	100	65	62	3	20	15
Beauty culture	31	100	81	81	—	16	3

NOTE.—Programs with fewer than 25 labor-market entrants among the youth surveyed are excluded except from city totals.

Table 27.—Percent Distribution of Trained St. Louis Labor-Market Entrants, by Selected Program, Completion of Training, and Employment Status in Relation to Vocational Training

Program	Youth with completed training					Training incomplete				
	Total		With related jobs	With unrelated jobs	With no jobs of 15 hours or more per week	Total		With related jobs	With unrelated jobs	With no jobs of 15 hours or more per week
	Number	Percent				Number	Percent			
St. Louis	829	100	75	15	10	1,525	100	51	43	6
Commercial programs	542	100	76	13	11	806	100	55	37	8
General commercial	38	100	55	24	21	226	100	44	48	8
General business	40	100	60	20	20	101	100	51	40	9
Stenography	90	100	87	10	3	147	100	54	41	5
Secretarial	193	100	75	10	15	87	100	64	23	13
Special commercial	138	100	80	13	7	152	100	75	14	11
Industrial programs	169	100	76	18	6	530	100	47	50	3
Auto mechanics	30	100	70	20	10	84	100	49	47	4
Electricity	40	100	85	10	5	105	100	47	48	5
Machine shop	33	100	82	15	3	79	100	72	27	1
Women's programs	87	100	69	16	15	129	100	44	44	12
Industrial sewing	31	100	45	32	23	72	100	47	49	4
Arts programs	31	100	61	36	3	60	100	47	51	2
Commercial art	28	100	64	32	4	26	100	54	42	4

NOTE.—Programs with fewer than 25 youth in either group—complete or incomplete training—are excluded except from the totals and subtotals.

Table 28.—Percent Distribution of St. Louis Trained Labor-Market Entrants According to Relationship of Job to Training, by Selected Program and by Race

Program and race	Total St. Louis labor-market entrants	Work histories of youth according to relationship of jobs to training (percent distribution)					
		Total	Related	Primary relationship	Secondary relationship only	No relationship	No jobs of 15 hours or more per week
Total youth	2,354	100	59	47	12	33	8
White	2,250	100	60	47	13	34	6
Negro	104	100	35	33	2	26	39
Commercial programs	1,348	100	63	50	13	28	9
White	1,308	100	65	51	14	27	8
Negro	40	100	23	20	3	35	42
Women's programs	216	100	54	51	3	33	13
White	168	100	55	51	4	39	6
Negro	48	100	52	52	—	13	35

Table 29.—Employment Status in Relation to Vocational Training, of Trained Youth Who Graduated From the Eighth Grade in 1929, by Month and by Sex, July 1930–July 1938

Year and month	Both sexes					Male					Female				
	Total number in labor market	Total	Employed in field of training	Employed in other fields	Unemployed [1]	Total number in labor market	Total	Employed in field of training	Employed in other fields	Unemployed [1]	Total number in labor market	Total	Employed in field of training	Employed in other fields	Unemployed [1]
			Percent					Percent					Percent		
1930															
July	68	100	16	57	27	35	100	14	75	11	33	100	18	39	43
August	70	100	17	57	26	35	100	14	75	11	35	100	20	40	40
September	70	100	19	52	29	35	100	14	72	14	35	100	23	34	43
October	68	100	19	60	21	34	100	15	73	12	34	100	24	47	29
November	73	100	22	57	21	34	100	15	76	9	39	100	28	41	31
December	76	100	22	56	22	37	100	16	73	11	39	100	28	39	33
1931															
January	78	100	18	51	31	38	100	16	66	18	40	100	20	37	43
February	93	100	26	45	29	44	100	25	59	16	49	100	26	33	41
March	96	100	25	47	28	46	100	24	59	17	50	100	26	36	38
April	100	100	26	47	27	47	100	23	58	19	53	100	28	38	34
May	110	100	26	48	26	50	100	24	66	10	60	100	27	33	40
June	118	100	25	48	27	56	100	23	59	18	62	100	25	34	41
July	158	100	23	44	33	70	100	20	56	24	88	100	25	36	39
August	158	100	24	44	32	70	100	23	53	24	88	100	26	32	42
September	160	100	24	42	34	70	100	23	54	23	90	100	28	38	34
October	166	100	26	43	31	68	100	23	52	25	98	100	26	39	35
November	167	100	25	44	31	68	100	23	52	25	99	100	26	38	36
December	171	100	26	44	30	71	100	23	52	25	100	100	28	39	33
1932															
January	171	100	26	43	31	70	100	23	50	27	101	100	28	38	34
February	190	100	26	44	30	75	100	20	51	29	115	100	30	39	31
March	189	100	25	45	30	75	100	20	52	28	114	100	29	39	32
April	192	100	26	46	28	78	100	19	55	26	114	100	31	40	29
May	207	100	25	45	30	82	100	20	57	23	125	100	29	36	35
June	214	100	24	45	31	87	100	19	58	23	127	100	28	35	37
July	277	100	22	41	37	109	100	19	55	26	168	100	24	31	45
August	279	100	22	41	37	111	100	18	54	28	168	100	25	32	43
September	280	100	23	41	36	112	100	18	54	28	168	100	27	32	41
October	278	100	25	42	33	109	100	19	55	26	169	100	30	33	37
November	282	100	28	43	29	109	100	21	55	24	173	100	32	35	33
December	292	100	28	44	28	117	100	20	59	21	175	100	33	34	33
1933															
January	293	100	29	42	29	117	100	19	58	23	176	100	35	32	33
February	344	100	27	42	31	144	100	18	55	27	200	100	34	32	34
March	344	100	27	44	29	144	100	19	57	24	200	100	32	35	33
April	353	100	28	46	26	145	100	19	60	21	208	100	34	36	30
May	360	100	28	45	27	145	100	20	59	21	215	100	34	35	31
June	366	100	28	43	29	149	100	20	57	23	217	100	35	33	32
July	484	100	24	38	38	198	100	20	50	30	286	100	27	29	44
August	486	100	25	39	36	201	100	21	51	28	285	100	28	31	41
September	485	100	27	41	32	200	100	21	52	27	285	100	30	33	37
October	484	100	27	40	33	195	100	22	49	29	289	100	30	34	36
November	488	100	28	39	33	195	100	22	47	31	293	100	32	34	34
December	498	100	28	39	33	197	100	23	49	28	301	100	32	33	35
1934															
January	500	100	28	40	32	201	100	23	49	28	299	100	32	33	35
February	535	100	28	37	35	227	100	23	44	33	308	100	32	32	36
March	537	100	30	37	33	228	100	25	45	30	309	100	33	32	35
April	538	100	30	38	32	233	100	23	47	30	305	100	35	31	34
May	551	100	30	39	31	240	100	23	48	29	311	100	36	31	33
June	573	100	30	39	31	247	100	23	51	26	326	100	35	31	34
July	678	100	29	36	35	283	100	23	48	30	395	100	34	29	37
August	677	100	29	36	35	284	100	23	47	30	393	100	34	28	38
September	683	100	30	37	33	287	100	23	49	28	396	100	36	28	36
October	663	100	32	39	29	276	100	25	51	24	387	100	38	29	33
November	667	100	33	39	28	279	100	23	53	24	388	100	40	30	30
December	675	100	33	39	28	281	100	23	53	24	394	100	40	30	30

See footnote at end of table.

Table 29.—Employment Status in Relation to Vocational Training, of Trained Youth Who Graduated from the Eighth Grade in 1929, by Month and by Sex, July 1930–July 1938—Continued

Year and month	Both sexes					Male					Female				
	Total number in labor market	Total	Employed in field of training	Employed in other fields	Unemployed [1]	Total number in labor market	Total	Employed in field of training	Employed in other fields	Unemployed [1]	Total number in labor market	Total	Employed in field of training	Employed in other fields	Unemployed [1]
1935															
January	676	100	33	40	27	282	100	23	53	24	394	100	40	31	29
February	693	100	33	39	28	290	100	22	50	28	403	100	40	31	29
March	694	100	32	40	28	292	100	21	52	27	402	100	40	32	28
April	699	100	34	40	26	295	100	22	51	27	404	100	43	31	26
May	713	100	36	39	25	302	100	24	52	24	411	100	44	30	26
June	723	100	38	38	24	306	100	27	51	22	417	100	45	29	26
July	774	100	37	37	26	328	100	26	50	24	446	100	45	28	27
August	770	100	37	38	25	327	100	27	52	21	443	100	45	28	27
September	768	100	39	37	24	328	100	28	51	21	440	100	46	28	26
October	765	100	41	37	22	329	100	30	51	19	436	100	48	28	24
November	766	100	41	37	22	328	100	30	50	20	438	100	50	27	23
December	768	100	42	36	22	327	100	31	49	20	441	100	50	27	23
1936															
January	771	100	42	38	20	328	100	31	50	19	443	100	51	28	21
February	769	100	42	38	20	327	100	31	50	19	442	100	51	28	21
March	771	100	43	38	19	329	100	31	51	18	442	100	52	28	20
April	776	100	43	39	18	331	100	31	54	15	445	100	52	28	20
May	771	100	45	39	16	332	100	33	54	13	439	100	53	28	19
June	773	100	45	39	16	334	100	34	54	12	439	100	54	27	19
July	783	100	46	39	15	339	100	33	56	11	444	100	55	27	18
August	782	100	46	39	15	337	100	35	55	10	445	100	55	27	18
September	781	100	47	39	14	335	100	35	54	11	446	100	57	27	16
October	773	100	48	38	14	336	100	36	53	11	437	100	56	27	17
November	777	100	48	39	13	335	100	36	54	10	442	100	57	28	15
December	777	100	48	39	13	337	100	37	53	10	440	100	56	29	15
1937															
January	778	100	48	40	12	340	100	36	54	10	438	100	57	30	13
February	778	100	49	40	11	338	100	38	52	10	440	100	59	30	11
March	778	100	50	39	11	340	100	39	52	9	438	100	58	30	12
April	778	100	50	39	11	341	100	39	52	9	437	100	59	29	12
May	776	100	50	39	11	342	100	39	53	8	434	100	59	28	13
June	779	100	51	39	10	343	100	41	53	6	436	100	59	28	13
July	775	100	50	39	11	348	100	40	52	8	427	100	58	28	14
August	774	100	50	39	11	348	100	40	51	9	426	100	59	28	13
September	770	100	50	38	12	346	100	40	51	9	424	100	59	27	14
October	768	100	51	38	11	341	100	40	52	8	427	100	59	27	14
November	769	100	52	37	11	341	100	41	51	8	428	100	60	27	13
December	768	100	51	37	12	342	100	40	49	11	426	100	61	26	13
1938															
January	763	100	50	37	13	339	100	37	50	13	424	100	60	27	13
February	764	100	49	37	14	340	100	37	48	15	424	100	59	27	14
March	764	100	49	37	14	341	100	36	50	14	423	100	59	27	14
April	762	100	49	37	14	341	100	35	50	15	421	100	59	26	15
May	762	100	48	38	14	341	100	35	52	13	421	100	58	27	15
June	758	100	47	38	15	340	100	34	52	14	418	100	58	27	15
July	765	100	46	39	15	347	100	33	52	15	418	100	57	27	16

[1] Includes youth employed less than 15 hours per week.

Table 30.—Employment Status in Relation to Vocational Training, of Trained Youth Who Graduated From the Eighth Grade in 1933, by Month and by Sex, July 1934–July 1938

[4 Cities]

Year and month	Both sexes				Male				Female			
	Total number in labor market	Employed in field of training	Employed in other fields	Unemployed[1]	Total number in labor market	Employed in field of training	Employed in other fields	Unemployed[1]	Total number in labor market	Employed in field of training	Employed in other fields	Unemployed[1]
1934												
July	46	2	44	54	29	—	48	52	17	*	*	*
August	46	2	44	54	29	—	48	52	17	*	*	*
September	45	4	40	56	28	—	46	54	17	*	*	*
October	37	5	49	46	25	—	56	44	12	*	*	*
November	39	5	54	41	27	—	59	41	12	*	*	*
December	41	5	49	46	27	—	56	44	14	*	*	*
1935												
January	44	5	59	36	30	—	63	37	14	*	*	*
February	62	13	51	36	42	14	60	26	20	*	*	*
March	67	13	51	36	43	14	60	26	24	*	*	*
April	76	17	47	36	49	16	53	31	27	19	37	44
May	89	15	52	33	59	14	57	29	30	17	43	40
June	102	16	47	37	67	16	54	30	35	14	34	52
July	154	16	40	44	95	18	45	37	59	14	31	55
August	155	17	39	44	96	20	45	35	59	14	29	57
September	156	17	40	43	95	21	46	33	61	12	29	59
October	161	19	40	41	101	23	46	31	60	12	30	58
November	169	19	42	39	108	22	48	30	61	13	31	56
December	182	20	44	36	119	24	48	28	63	13	35	52
1936												
January	186	22	43	35	122	25	45	30	64	14	39	47
February	211	21	41	38	139	23	42	35	72	17	39	44
March	221	22	41	37	145	24	43	33	76	17	40	43
April	241	24	40	36	156	26	42	32	85	19	38	43
May	256	25	41	34	168	28	43	29	88	19	38	43
June	283	27	41	32	188	30	44	26	95	21	36	43
July	342	30	38	32	210	34	43	23	132	24	29	47
August	344	32	41	27	212	35	45	20	132	27	34	39
September	345	32	40	28	213	35	44	21	132	27	36	37
October	348	35	44	21	214	36	47	17	134	34	38	28
November	355	34	45	21	217	35	48	17	138	34	39	27
December	362	35	45	20	221	35	47	18	141	34	43	23
1937												
January	368	35	45	20	222	37	47	16	146	34	41	25
February	405	35	43	22	244	36	46	18	161	32	41	27
March	406	36	44	20	246	38	46	16	160	33	42	25
April	414	37	43	20	248	38	46	16	166	34	40	26
May	424	38	44	18	254	40	47	13	170	35	40	25
June	430	38	45	17	257	41	48	11	173	32	40	28
July	560	36	38	26	320	41	43	16	240	30	30	40
August	564	38	37	25	321	42	44	14	243	33	28	39
September	567	39	38	23	322	41	43	16	245	36	31	33
October	566	41	38	21	321	43	43	14	245	37	32	31
November	572	40	37	23	323	42	43	15	249	38	29	33
December	573	40	37	23	322	42	42	16	251	38	30	32
1938												
January	572	40	37	23	323	41	42	17	249	38	31	31
February	596	38	33	29	334	39	38	23	262	36	27	37
March	596	38	34	28	337	39	39	22	259	38	26	36
April	602	39	34	27	339	39	40	21	263	39	27	34
May	610	39	35	26	342	38	42	20	268	41	27	32
June	616	37	36	27	349	35	43	22	267	40	25	35
July	718	34	31	35	382	33	41	26	336	35	21	44

* Percentages not calculated on base of less than 25.

[1] Includes youth employed less than 15 hours per week.

Table 31.—First Full-Time Jobs and Full-Time Jobs Held on July 1, 1938, by Vocation-ally Trained Youth, According to Relationship of Job to Training, by City and Completion of Training

City and completion of training	First full-time jobs [1]					Final full-time jobs [1]				
		Percent distribution of jobs according to relationship of job to training					Percent distribution of jobs according to relationship of job to training			
	Number	Total	Primary relation-ship	Secondary relation-ship	No relation-ship	Number	Total	Primary relation-ship	Secondary relation-ship	No relation-ship
4 cities	2,599	100	36	13	51	1,862	100	41	14	45
Smith-Hughes complete	958	100	53	14	33	738	100	58	15	27
Smith-Hughes incomplete	1,641	100	27	12	61	1,124	100	29	13	58
St. Louis	2,149	100	38	13	49	1,565	100	41	15	44
Smith-Hughes complete	730	100	56	15	29	575	100	61	16	23
Smith-Hughes incomplete	1,419	100	28	12	60	990	100	30	14	56
Birmingham	191	100	25	15	60	127	100	26	12	62
Smith-Hughes complete	91	100	34	17	49	63	100	30	16	54
Smith-Hughes incomplete	100	100	16	14	70	64	100	22	18	60
Denver	63	100	16	13	71	52	100	15	8	77
Smith-Hughes complete	20	100	35	15	50	18	100	28	6	66
Smith-Hughes incomplete	43	100	7	12	81	34	100	9	9	82
Seattle	196	100	41	7	52	118	100	61	9	30
Smith-Hughes complete	117	100	56	5	39	82	100	71	7	22
Smith-Hughes incomplete	79	100	20	9	71	36	100	39	14	47

[1] Youth with 1 job only are included in both groups.

Table 32.—First Full-Time Jobs and Full-Time Jobs Held on July 1, 1938, by St. Louis Vocationally Trained Youth, According to Relationship of Job to Training, by Selected Training Program and Completion of Training

City, program, and completion of training	First full-time jobs [1]					Final full-time jobs [1]				
		Percent distribution of jobs according to relationship of job to training					Percent distribution of jobs according to relationship of job to training			
	Number	Total	Primary relationship	Secondary relationship	No relationship	Number	Total	Primary relationship	Secondary relationship	No relationship
St. Louis	2,149	100	38	13	49	1,565	100	41	15	44
General business	122	100	50	5	45	87	100	56	5	39
Complete	32	100	66	3	31	24	†	†	†	†
Incomplete	90	100	44	6	50	63	100	49	3	48
Special commercial	261	100	57	18	25	186	100	73	11	16
Complete	126	100	71	13	16	98	100	78	10	12
Incomplete	135	100	45	22	33	88	100	68	11	21
Secretarial	241	100	47	17	36	203	100	58	23	19
Complete	164	100	48	21	31	144	100	58	24	18
Incomplete	77	100	47	9	44	59	100	58	19	23
Stenography	224	100	31	28	41	159	100	38	29	33
Complete	87	100	45	30	25	70	100	50	31	19
Incomplete	137	100	22	26	52	89	100	28	27	45
Machine shop	109	100	46	16	38	86	100	38	17	45
Complete	32	100	75	9	16	26	100	65	4	31
Incomplete	77	100	34	19	47	60	100	27	23	50
Electricity	135	100	27	7	66	106	100	34	9	57
Complete	37	100	62	8	30	30	100	63	13	24
Incomplete	98	100	13	7	80	76	100	22	8	70
Auto mechanics	107	100	25	18	57	79	100	19	23	58
Complete	26	100	42	23	35	21	†	†	†	†
Incomplete	81	100	20	16	64	58	100	10	28	62
Cosmetology	40	100	85	—	15	33	100	82	—	18
Complete	38	100	87	—	13	31	100	84	—	16
Incomplete	2	†	†	†	†	2	†	†	†	†

†Number too small for percentage distribution.

[1] Youth with 1 job only are included in both groups.

NOTE.— Programs with fewer than 25 youth in first jobs are excluded except from the totals.

Table 33.—Average Duration of Full-Time Jobs, by Relationship of Job to Training and by Completion of Training, Selected Training Programs, by City

City and program	All jobs	First of 2 jobs or more	Last of 2 jobs[1] or more	Primary relationship	No relationship	Complete	Incomplete
				Relationship of job to training		Smith-Hughes training	
St. Louis	8	6	17	9	6	8	7
Commercial programs	8	5	19	11	5	9	7
General commercial	7	6	23	10	5	9	7
General business	7	4	16	12	5	8	7
Stenography	8	5	21	10	7	9	8
Accounting	10	†	†	8	10	7	14
Clerical	7	5	†	10	5	†	6
Secretarial	8	4	17	9	5	9	6
Special commercial	8	5	16	12	4	12	6
Industrial programs	8	8	16	9	8	7	8
Aeromechanics	4	†	†	†	4	3	8
Drafting	9	11	18	—	9	6	10
Auto mechanics	8	8	15	10	6	9	8
Electricity	8	8	17	12	6	10	7
Machine shop	8	9	16	10	7	11	7
Printing	9	8	17	7	11	6	10
Sheet metal	10	9	20	†	11	†	10
Woodworking	10	9	15	†	9	†	10
Women's programs	6	7	12	5	6	6	5
Cafeteria-tearoom	7	11	†	†	10	†	8
Cosmetology	7	7	†	8	†	7	†
Industrial sewing	5	6	13	5	5	6	5
Arts programs	7	6	13	8	7	5	9
Commercial art	6	3	†	8	4	4	9
Show-card writing	9	9	†	†	8	†	9
Birmingham	5	5	13	5	5	4	5
Retailing	2	†	†	†	3	2	2
Denver	5	6	18	7	5	5	5
Auto mechanics	5	6	†	†	5	†	5
Seattle	4	3	12	5	3	4	3
Beauty culture	4	†	†	6	3	5	†
Business training	3	†	†	3	2	3	2

† Median duration not computed for fewer than 25 jobs.
[1] Includes only jobs held on July 1, 1938.
NOTE.—Programs with fewer than 25 registrants or with less than 50 jobs held by youth trained therein are excluded except from the totals and subtotals.

Table 34.—Average[1] Time in the Labor Market and Time Employed, St. Louis Youth Trained in Selected Smith-Hughes Programs

Program	Number of labor-market youth	Average[1] months in labor market	Average[1] months employed	Percent of labor-market time employed[3]
St. Louis	1,737	42	33	79
Secretarial	280	29	24	82
Stenography	237	44	36	81
Special commercial	290	38	29	76
General business	141	34	26	76
General commercial	264	53	40	75
Printing	80	49	42	86
Machine shop	112	42	35	83
Auto mechanics	114	46	37	82
Electricity	145	49	40	82
Woodworking	74	53	42	79

[1] Mean.
[3] Based on averages carried out to one decimal place.

Table 35.—Average [1] Weekly Earnings of Youth on Full-Time Jobs, by Relationship of Job to Training and by Completion of Training, Selected Training Programs, by City

City and program	Total number of full-time jobs	Average [1] weekly earnings of youth on all full-time jobs						
		All jobs	First of 2 jobs or more	Last of 2 jobs [2] or more	Relationship of job to training		Smith-Hughes training	
					Primary relationship	No relationship	Complete	Incomplete
St. Louis	5,223	$14.70	$12.80	$16.30	$14.90	$14.20	$14.60	$14.70
Commercial programs	2,752	14.20	12.60	15.40	14.80	13.30	14.50	14.10
General commercial	607	13.20	11.70	14.80	14.50	12.80	11.60	13.40
General business	258	14.20	12.90	15.10	14.80	13.40	14.00	14.30
Stenography	535	14.10	11.90	15.40	14.60	13.00	14.30	13.90
Accounting	79	16.40	14.80	†	15.30	16.80	15.70	17.70
Clerical	114	13.30	11.80	†	13.20	13.30	†	13.30
Secretarial	503	14.80	13.70	15.80	14.90	13.90	14.80	15.00
Special commercial	551	14.60	12.50	15.40	14.90	14.30	14.60	14.60
Industrial programs	1,781	16.20	14.10	19.10	16.90	15.40	16.00	16.20
Aeromechanics	87	16.00	14.90	†	†	15.10	15.40	16.40
Drafting	145	17.40	15.00	19.90	†	16.10	16.70	17.80
Auto mechanics	296	16.70	14.50	17.90	18.10	15.50	17.70	16.50
Electricity	377	16.80	14.60	20.10	18.40	15.90	16.70	16.90
Machine shop	310	16.20	14.40	18.70	17.30	15.20	16.20	16.30
Printing	199	14.90	13.20	18.60	13.60	15.40	14.70	15.10
Sheet metal	138	15.90	13.40	20.00	†	15.50	†	15.90
Woodworking	173	16.30	12.80	21.50	†	15.70	†	16.20
Women's programs	496	12.40	11.00	14.00	12.40	12.40	11.30	13.00
Cafeteria-tearoom	92	12.70	12.10	†	†	13.50	†	13.10
Cosmetology	88	10.60	10.00	†	10.40	†	10.70	†
Industrial sewing	292	13.00	11.20	14.10	14.00	12.10	11.70	13.20
Arts programs	194	15.10	13.60	19.90	15.10	14.70	15.00	15.10
Commercial arts	104	14.60	13.20	†	15.20	13.70	15.10	13.70
Show-card writing	81	15.40	14.50	21.50	†	15.10	†	15.50
Birmingham	614	15.40	12.40	18.30	16.10	15.30	16.00	15.00
Retailing	82	13.00	†	†	†	15.00	13.60	10.70
Denver	211	15.30	13.70	19.20	13.50	15.30	15.40	15.20
Auto mechanics	126	15.30	13.00	†	†	15.30	†	15.30
Seattle	592	15.10	13.80	18.60	15.00	15.10	15.00	15.30
Beauty culture	79	13.20	†	†	11.70	13.80	13.00	†
Business training	89	14.70	†	†	15.30	13.30	14.80	14.60

†Average not computed for fewer than 25 jobs.

[1] Median, to nearest 10 cents.
[2] Includes only jobs held on July 1, 1938.

NOTE.—Programs with fewer than 25 registrants are excluded except from the totals and subtotals.

Table 36.—Comparison of Criteria of Measuring Success of Vocationally Trained Youth in the Labor Market, Selected Programs in St. Louis

Program	Selected criteria of success			
	Percent of labor-market time employed	Percent of labor-market youth ever employed in related field	Duration of all full-time jobs (in months)	Average weekly earnings on all full-time jobs
St. Louis	79	59	7	$14.70
Secretarial	82	72	7	14.80
Stenography	81	66	8	14.10
Special commercial	76	78	8	14.60
General business	76	54	7	14.20
General commercial	75	46	7	13.20
Printing	86	59	9	14.90
Machine shop	83	75	8	16.20
Auto mechanics	82	54	3	16.70
Electricity	82	57	7	16.80
Woodworking	79	30	9	16.30

Table 37.—Percent Distribution of Seattle Labor-Market Entrants With Regular High-School Vocational Training, by Selected Training Program and by Relationship of Job to Training

Program	Total labor-market entrants with regular high-school vocational training	Percent distribution of youth according to relationship of job to training				
		Total	One related job or more		No jobs related to training	No jobs of 15 hours or more per week
			Total	Primary relationship	Secondary relationship		
Seattle	1,178	100	51	37	14	43	6
1 program only	920	100	50	37	13	43	7
Retail selling	44	100	77	70	7	21	2
General clerking	182	100	54	49	5	37	9
Stenography	365	100	62	44	18	30	8
Bookkeeping	31	100	55	39	16	42	3
Metal shop	50	100	48	32	16	46	6
Woodshop	122	100	26	13	13	70	4
Drafting	49	100	29	10	19	67	4
Art	62	100	16	8	8	74	10
2 programs	232	100	53	40	13	42	5
Bookkeeping and stenography	25	100	60	40	20	36	4
Metal shop and woodshop	50	100	50	32	18	46	4
Bookkeeping and general clerking	25	100	32	28	4	64	4
3 programs or more	26	100	58	35	23	42	—

NOTE.—Programs with fewer than 25 registrants are excluded except from totals and subtotals.

Table 38.—Average Weekly Earnings on Full-Time Jobs Held by Seattle Youth With Regular High-School Vocational Training, by Selected Training Program and by Relationship of Job to Training

Program	Total number of full-time jobs	Full-time jobs held by Seattle youth with regular high-school vocational training			
		All full-time jobs	Relationship of job to training		
			Primary relationship	Secondary relationship	No relationship
Full-time jobs:					
Number	3,129	[1] 3,129	720	362	2,047
Percent	100	100	23	12	65
		Average [2] weekly earnings			
Seattle	3,129	$16.40	$16.30	$16.10	$16.50
1 program only	2,389	15.90	16.10	15.50	15.90
Retail selling	98	15.10	16.20	†	14.20
General clerking	456	14.90	15.40	15.90	14.50
Stenography	802	14.90	15.90	15.10	14.00
Bookkeeping	68	16.50	†	†	17.60
Metal shop	190	20.00	20.00	†	19.80
Woodshop	421	19.60	21.50	†	19.50
Drafting	160	20.00	†	†	20.00
Art	137	15.40	†	†	15.50
2 programs	649	18.00	16.70	19.50	18.30
Bookkeeping and stenography	59	15.20	†	†	14.70
Metal shop and woodshop	164	19.60	†	†	19.00
Bookkeeping and general clerking	63	17.70	†	†	17.90
3 programs or more	91	19.70	†	†	19.90

†Averages not computed for fewer than 25 jobs.

[1] Includes 31 jobs with earnings not ascertainable and 19 jobs with no earnings, which are excluded from all figures on average earnings.

[2] Median, rounded to nearest 10 cents.

NOTE.—Programs with fewer than 25 labor-market entrants are excluded except from the totals and subtotals.

Table 39.—Evaluation of Assistance Received From Vocational Training by St. Louis Youth, by Selected Training Program

Program	Total youth ques-tioned	Percent of youth assisted by vocational training					
		In securing job			On the job		
		All youth who had held jobs	Youth with completed training	Youth with uncom-pleted training	All youth who had held jobs	Youth with completed training	Youth with uncom-pleted training
St. Louis	¹ 1,472	52	75	40	60	80	51
Commercial programs	829	57	76	46	64	81	54
General commercial	148	38	†	34	44	†	40
General business	80	45	†	39	60	†	53
Stenography	154	62	88	49	69	92	58
Accounting	29	59	†	†	69	†	†
Clerical	40	25	†	22	40	†	38
Secretarial	168	73	74	70	79	81	74
Special commercial	186	67	75	60	73	80	67
Industrial programs	457	44	77	35	54	80	48
Aeromechanics	29	41	†	29	55	†	48
Drafting	38	45	†	28	53·	†	44
Auto mechanics	76	41	†	36	53	†	48
Electricity	91	47	91	32	54	91	41
Machine shop	69	61	†	53	74	†	69
Printing	56	64	†	62	68	†	67
Sheet metal	37	24	†	24	38	†	38
Woodworking	48	17	†	15	37	†	35
Women's programs	128	50	73	30	56	78	38
Cosmetology	33	91	91	†	94	94	†
Industrial sewing	61	47	52	45	53	57	50
Arts programs	58	53	71	43	52	62	46
Commercial art	32	63	†	†	63	†	†

† Percent not calculated on base of less than 25.

¹ Excludes 141 youth who had never held jobs and 2 youth whose answers to questions regarding assistance from vocational training were not ascertainable.

NOTE.—Based on a partial sample of the trained youth who were interviewed. All programs with fewer than 25 youth responding to these questions are excluded except from the totals and subtotals.

Table 40.—Criticisms of Vocational Training by Trained Youth, by Completion of Training, and by City

| Criticism of training received | Total | Smith-Hughes training | | St Louis | Birmingham | Denver | Seattle |
		Completed	Uncompleted*				
Youth questioned	[1] 1,793	622	1,171	1,550	72	55	116
Worth while	851	343	508	713	42	27	69
No criticisms	542	161	381	519	5	1	17
With definite criticisms	400	118	282	318	25	27	30
			Percent distribution				
Youth questioned	100	100	100	100	100	100	100
Worth while	48	55	43	46	58	49	59
No criticisms	30	26	33	33	7	2	15
With definite criticisms	22	19	24	21	35	49	26
			Percent distribution				
Youth with definite criticisms	100	100	100	100	100	100	100
Incompleteness	16	24	13	15	12	22	23
Lack of equipment	11	8	13	10	20	11	20
Too much theory	7	6	8	6	16	15	3
Standards too low	5	6	4	4	—	7	7
Lack of teachers	4	3	5	4	4	11	—
Program too short	3	4	2	2	12	4	7
Miscellaneous	54	49	55	59	36	30	40

[1] Excludes 6 youth whose training status was not ascertainable.

NOTE.—Based on a partial sample of the trained youth who were interviewed.

Appendix B

LIST OF TABLES

Index

INDEX

149

○